CASH
-SECURED
PUT OPTIONS
for
WEEKLY PAYDAYS

EARN SAFE, STEADY INCOME
IN ALL MARKET CONDITIONS -
—— EVEN WITH ——
A SMALL ACCOUNT

FREEMAN PUBLICATIONS

TABLE OF CONTENTS

WANT TO LEARN MORE?

We regularly post videos on our YouTube channel, covering strategies, deep dives, and insights to help you go even further on your financial journey.

Whether you are just getting started or looking to sharpen your skills, you will find something valuable there.

To explore more, scan the QR code below or visit:

freemanpublications.com/youtube

HOW TO GET THE MOST OUT OF THIS BOOK

All of these bonuses are 100% free, with no strings attached. You don't need to enter any details except your email address.

To get your bonuses scan the QR code below or go to

https://freemanpublications.com/bonus

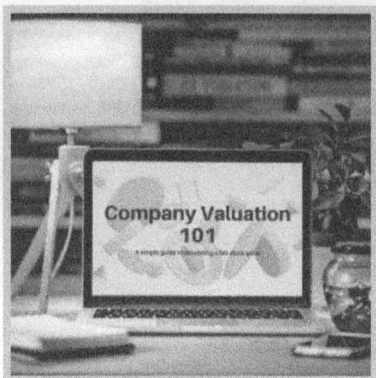

Free bonus #1: Company Valuation 101 video course ($97 value)

In this 8 part video course you'll see my process for profitably trading the wheel. This will give you an over the shoulder look at the entire strategy, plus see me trading live in real time, with real results.

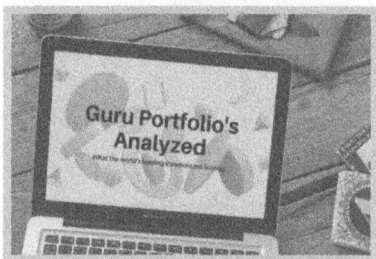

Free bonus #2: Guru Portfolios Analyzed ($37 value)

In these videos, we analyze the stock portfolios of Billionaire investors like Warren Buffett. As well as top entrepreneurs like Bill Gates.

Free bonus #3: 4 "Backdoor" Ways to Profit from Cryptocurrency ($47 value)

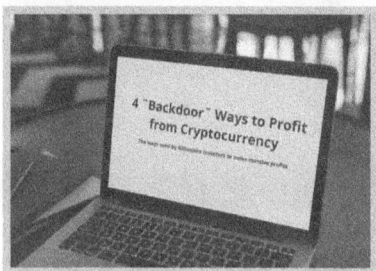

When you have a paradigm-shifting technology like cryptocurrency and blockchain ... there are multiple ways to profit from it.

But before you rush out and buy every altcoin under the sun... there is a smarter way of doing this.

The ways used by hedge funds and Billionaire investors to make massive profits from the price of Bitcoin and other cryptocurrencies.

And you don't need anything more than a regular brokerage account to do so.

We covered exactly how to do this in a private call for our premium members recently and you ll get access to this video for free.

Free bonus #4: 2 Stocks to Sell Right Now ($17 value)

These 2 stocks are in danger of plummeting in the next 12 months. They're both popular with retail investors, and one is even in the top 5 most held stocks on Robinhood. Believe us; you don't want to be holding these going into 2025 and beyond.

Free bonus #5: AI Disruptor - The $4 Stock Poised to be the Next Big Thing in Computing ($17 value)

This under the radar company, which less than 1% of investors have heard of, is at the forefront of a breakthrough technology that will change our lives as we know them. Soon this technology will be in every smartphone, tablet, and laptop on the planet.

Free bonus #6: Options 101 ($17 Value)

Options don't have to be risky. In fact, they were invented to *reduce* risk. It's no wonder that smart investors like Warren Buffett regularly use options to supplement their long-term portfolio. In this quick start guide, we show you how options work and why they are tools to be utilized rather than feared.

Free bonus #7: The 1 Dividend Stock to Buy and Hold for the Rest of Your Life ($17 Value)

Dividends are the lifeblood of any income investor, and this stock is a cornerstone of any dividend strategy. A true dividend aristocrat with consistent payouts for over 50 years which you'll want to add to your portfolio for sure.

INTRODUCTION

L et me guess.

You've heard about people getting rich in the stock market and thought "I want a piece of the action."

So you started buying stocks when you thought they'd go up... and selling before they crashed down.

How'd that work out for you?

If you're like most people, reality hit you like a freight train the moment you put real money on the line.

Here's the thing though...

My answer to "How do I make money in the stock market?" has always been the same.

Buy quality companies. Hold them for the long term. Maybe throw in some gold or Bitcoin to hedge against inflation.

But what if that's not enough?

What if you're staring at your retirement account thinking "There's no way this gets me to where I need to be"?

Or maybe you've got a decent nest egg but you're confused about what to do with it beyond parking it in a high-yield savings account or handing it over to some advisor who'll charge you insane fees to deliver mediocre returns.

That's where Cash Secured Puts come in.

Now before you roll your eyes and think "Great, another options guru trying to sell me the dream"... hear me out.

Most people think options are just gambling instruments for day traders.

They're wrong.

When used correctly, Cash Secured Puts are simple, reliable, and incredibly effective for generating income while acquiring quality stocks at a discount.

Think about it this way.

You get paid while positioning yourself to buy stocks you actually want to own.

For decades, bonds and dividend stocks were the only "safe" income sources.

But Cash Secured Puts can make you just as much money (if not more) than dividends... with a much smaller capital base... all while building positions in quality companies.

The catch?

This approach requires patience.

You need to be willing to slowly compound your money instead of chasing those "200%+ returns every year" day trading fantasies that'll blow up your account.

In my view, minimizing risk is far more important than shooting for huge gains.

Anyone can generate 100% returns if they're willing to risk 150% per trade. But generating 15-30% annual returns while risking just a small percentage of your capital on any given trade? That's the real skill.

And that's exactly what this strategy does.

The approach in this book focuses on Cash Secured Puts as a simple, conservative options strategy.

You'll learn to construct a portfolio that generates 15-30% additional annual income while acquiring quality stocks below market value.

Is it low risk? Yes.

Is it boring? Some would say so.

But when it comes to the stock market, boring beats exciting every single time.

The real power lies in generating income consistently without taking on additional risk.

Whether you have $10,000 or $1 million, this strategy scales.

And before you think this is some untested theory I cooked up in my basement...

Warren Buffett routinely sells puts to generate income for Berkshire Hathaway (despite calling derivatives "financial weapons of mass destruction").

Ed Thorp's Princeton Newport Partners (the original "hedge fund") averaged 22% annually over 20 years trading options, without a single down year. That's a 14.5x return.

Now I'm not claiming you can turn pocket change into millions.

But this strategy has the potential to generate an additional 15-30% annually without additional portfolio risk while positioning you to acquire quality companies at attractive prices.

I've used this strategy in my own life and worked with hundreds of others to do the same.

I've taught people from 19 to 83 years old.

My hope is that this book encourages you to begin your own Cash Secured Put journey so you can prosper financially and live an extraordinary retired life.

If at any time, you'd like help implementing what's inside, book a call with me or my team at: https://investingcoach.com/work-with-me

We work with people like you every day, helping them get their options portfolios up and running.

Oliver El-Gorr

Founder and CEO

Freeman Publications

London, England - June 2025

Chapter 1

THE ANT, THE GRASSHOPPER, AND THE PROBLEM WITH TRADITIONAL RETIREMENT PLANNING

"The frog does not drink up the pond in which he lives."
- Native American Proverb.

L et me tell you about the phone call that kept me awake for 2 nights straight.

It was a Thursday afternoon in October 2023. I was reviewing some trade setups when my phone buzzed. On the other end was my friend Brett, a successful e-commerce agency owner who had built his business from scratch over the past eight years.

"Oliver," he said, and I could hear the exhaustion in his voice. "We just lost another client. That's three this month. They're all saying the same thing, they can get 80% of what we do with AI tools for 80% less cost. At this rate, we'll be out of business in two years."

Brett paused, and I heard him take a shaky breath before turning the topic to his 2 high school aged kids. "Sophia's a junior, Michael's a sophomore. They're both talking about which colleges they want to apply to, and I'm sitting here wondering how the hell I'm going to pay for any of it."

Brett was living the modern version of an old fable, the one about the ant and the grasshopper. You remember it, right? The ant spent all summer preparing for winter while the grasshopper enjoyed the sunshine. When winter came, the ant was ready. The grasshopper... well, it didn't end well for him.

Figure 1: The ant and the grasshopper (Source: Pinterest)

Here's the thing: Brett wasn't lazy or irresponsible. He'd built a successful agency and was doing everything the financial advisors tell you to do. He was maxing out his 401(k), had some money in index funds, and was even putting aside cash for the kids' college. He was trying to be the ant, but he was about to learn what millions of Americans are discovering the hard way.

Because How Much Is Really Enough?

Six months after that call, Brett came to me with a different problem. He'd managed to pivot his agency (we'll save that story for another time), but now he was obsessing over retirement numbers.

"Check out this article" his email said, linking to a Northwestern Mutual study that had been picked up by The Wall Street Journal.

"The average American needs $1.46 million for a comfortable retirement. Up from $1.25 million just two years ago."

Brett finished his email with "by the time I come to retire, who knows what the number will be?"

He had fallen into the same trap that catches most of us: treating retirement like a math problem to solve.

Think about all the formulas we're supposed to follow: The 10× salary rule (save 10 times your final salary), the 25× rule (save 25 times your annual expenses), or the 80% income replacement rule. Then there are the withdrawal strategies, asset allocation formulas, and budget rules. It's enough to make your head spin.

But here's what Brett, and most others, don't realize - retirement is not a math problem.

The Pain of Watching Your Nest Egg Shrink

Picture this: You've did everything the so-called-right-way for decades. You've said no to weekend trips, maxed out your retirement accounts, and stayed disciplined through every market crash. You finally hit your magic number and get permission to start withdrawing.

But as you make that first withdrawal, something strange happens. You feel sick to your stomach watching those numbers go down. All your life, you've been conditioned to see your portfolio go up and to the right. Now, without a paycheck to replenish it, every withdrawal feels like a real loss.

Psychologists call this "loss aversion", where we feel the pain of losing money about twice as intensely as the pleasure of gaining it. Remember how good the 25% rise in the S&P 500 felt? Now compare that to the gut-punch of the 15% drawdown we saw between February and April 2025. For many people, that kind of decline is enough to question capitalism itself.

This is why retirement planning is more of a human problem than a math puzzle.

The Reality Check: Traditional Income Sources Aren't Cutting It

Let's say you somehow manage to save that $1.46 million. What kind of income can you actually expect?

The average dividend yield of the S&P 500 over the last five years was about 1.46%. Do the math: $1.46 million × 1.46% = roughly $21,000 per year. That's barely above the poverty line.

"Okay," you might think, "I'll invest in high-dividend stocks." So you look at something like the Global X SuperDividend US ETF (DIV), which invests in the 50 highest dividend-yielding US stocks and currently yields about 5%. That would give you $73,000 annually on your $1.46 million, much better, right?

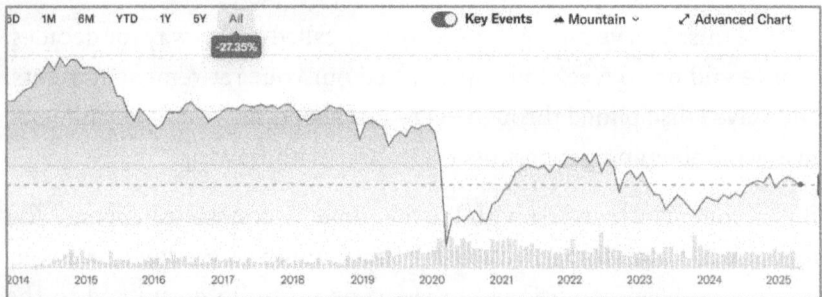

Figure 2: *Global X SuperDividend US ETF (DIV) historical price chart (Source: Yahoo Finance)*

Here's the catch: Since its inception, DIV has lost over 27% of its value. Even if you reinvested all dividends, it generated an average 10-year return of just 2.4%. You're getting income, but your principal is evaporating faster than ice cream in July.

High-yield savings accounts? The best ones are offering around 4.66% APY right now. With inflation at 3%, you're barely keeping up, and interest rates are likely heading down from here.

The Lazy Hopper's Revelation

This brings me back to Brett and our fable. Here's the part of the story they don't usually tell (because I'm making it up):

After that brutal winter, the Lazy Hopper (let's stick with that name) didn't just learn to save more grain. He realized something more important: winter could last longer than expected, and there would always be an ever-increasing need for food. So instead of relying on a fixed pile of grain to slowly nibble through, he figured out how to keep producing, even in winter.

The Lazy Hopper started growing his own grain to build a steady supply rather than depending on a single stockpile.

Many of us are just like the Lazy Hopper. We start saving late, not thinking much about retirement in our twenties, thirties, or even forties. Then suddenly we're faced with the inevitable pressure to catch up and build that magic retirement number. The prospect of working 60-hour weeks in our 60s and 70s hits hard.

But here's the good news: the Diligent Dan approach doesn't work for most people anyway.

Like the Lazy Hopper in the second part of our story, we need to approach retirement by focusing on income streams rather than just a lump sum. Retirement can last 30-40 years, market unpredictability isn't going away, and the cost of living will only increase.

We don't need to obsess over a nest egg that may not last. We can take a different approach: building steady, reliable income streams that work regardless of what the market does.

The Income First Solution

This book is about building one of those income streams—specifically, generating an additional 15-30% annual return (or more) through a low-risk options strategy that most people have never heard of.

But before we dive into that, let me address the elephant in the room: "Aren't options risky?"

That's exactly what Brett asked me six months after our first conversation. He'd stabilized his business, but he was still worried about building enough wealth for retirement and his kids' college expenses.

"I keep hearing about options," he said, "but isn't that just gambling?"

Let me demystify that for you in the next chapter.

Key takeaways

⬦ Traditional retirement planning doesn't work for most people. Saving a big lump sum sounds great in theory. However, real life is quite different from a financial spreadsheet.

⬦ Retirement isn't just a math puzzle. Loss aversion is real and painful. Watching your account go down feels worse than it ever felt good when it went up.

⬦ Most people don't have enough saved. The average retirement fund is nowhere close to the "magic number."

⬦ Dividend investing and high-yield savings aren't enough. They may bring in some income, but that's hardly enough to replace a paycheck.

⬦ It's better to build income streams than to rely on a single retirement fund.

Chapter 2

THE WORLD'S FIRST OPTION TRADE

"If you must play, decide on three things at the start: the rules of the game, the stakes, and the quitting time"
— Chinese Proverb.

Thales of Miletus (624 BC – 546 BC) was having a rough day at the ancient Greek equivalent of a coffee shop.

Picture this, here's one of the seven wisest men of ancient Greece... a brilliant philosopher, astronomer, and mathematician who had reached the highest levels of human knowledge. But his neighbors kept giving him grief about being broke.

"If you're so smart, Thales," they'd taunt, "why aren't you rich? What good is all that wisdom if it can't put food on the table?"

Sound familiar? It's the same question every academic, every deep thinker, every person who's more interested in understanding the world than making a quick buck has heard at some point.

Thales had had enough. He decided to prove them wrong.

Using his knowledge of astronomy and weather patterns, Thales predicted there would be a bumper crop of olives in the coming season. Now, here's where it gets interesting... and where Thales showed he understood something about leverage that most people miss even today.

He knew that a bigger olive harvest meant farmers would desperately need olive presses during harvest season. But instead of trying to buy or rent the presses outright (which would have cost him a fortune he didn't have), Thales did something clever.

He went to the olive press owners months before harvest season and made them an offer. He'd pay them a small fee now for the right to use their presses during harvest season... but only if he wanted to.

The press owners probably thought he was crazy. Easy money, right? They took his small payments and figured they'd never see him again.

When harvest season arrived, Thales' prediction proved correct. Olive production was through the roof, and suddenly every farmer in Miletus was desperately looking for press time. Supply and demand kicked in, and press rental prices skyrocketed.

But Thales had already locked in his rights for a fraction of the cost. He exercised those rights, rented out the press time at premium prices, and made a fortune.

Thousands of years before there was a stock ticker, Wall Street, or a trading app, Thales of Miletus had just executed what's now considered the world's first options contract.

Why This Story Matters (And Why Options Aren't What You Think)

Here's what I love about Thales' story, it perfectly illustrates why options don't have to be the risky, complicated instruments that financial media makes them out to be.

Let's break down what Thales actually did, because it's brilliant...

The Problem: He wanted to profit from his prediction, but buying or renting olive presses outright would have required massive capital he didn't have. Plus, if he was wrong, he'd lose everything.

The Solution: He paid small fees for the rights to use the presses, without the obligation to do so.

This arrangement gave him two huge advantages...

Limited risk: He only had to pay small fees upfront

No obligation: If his prediction was wrong, he could simply walk away, losing only those small fees

Without committing huge amounts of money, Thales could derive the same benefits as if he'd bought the presses outright. That's what options do: they give you choices without making huge commitments or taking substantial risks.

Let's take a modern example to understand this better.

Suppose Apple has just launched a substantially upgraded iPhone (after years of rotating the cameras and almost relaunching the same phone with higher price tags). You expect Apple to report better financial numbers in the next quarter and its stock price to go up substantially. However, buying the stock outright means you have to put in a substantial amount of money. Also, if your estimations go wrong, the stock can even go down in value.

 Now, what if you could pay a small fee (let's say 1 or 2% of the stock price) to lock the price at which you want to buy Apple stock within a certain future date, irrespective of the market price? If Apple stock goes up in the future, you can buy the stocks at the locked price and benefit from the price rise. However, if the stock goes down, you only lose the small fee. This is the beauty of options: they give you the right without an obligation in exchange for a small fee.

This takes us to the definition of options:

Options come in 2 kinds

◇ **Call options** give you the right to buy an asset.
◇ **Put options** give you the right to sell an asset.

Here's a snapshot of these two basic option types:

Expectations	Option type to use	What you get	Risk	Reward
Apple stock will go up.	Call options	The right to buy Apple stock at a set price within a specific date.	The small fee (called "premium") you pay.	Unlimited (the higher Apple stocks go, the larger your profit)
Tesla stock will go down.	Put options.	The right to sell Tesla stock at a set price within a specific date.	Premium paid.	Large, to the extent of the price decline.

Table 1: *Understanding Options*

As you can see from the examples above, you buy a call option when you're bullish on a stock and expect it to rise. (This also means someone with the opposite view is selling that call option to you.)

On the flip side, you buy a put option when you're bearish and expect the stock to fall. (Again, someone with the opposite view is selling that put to you.)

In this book, we're mainly going to focus on selling put options. It might sound complex, but I promise we'll break it down into simple, digestible pieces in the coming chapters.

Now, let's see how this works in the real world with some actual numbers:

Example 1: Call options on Apple Inc. (AAPL)

As of April 4, 2025, Apple's stock is trading at $188.38. Let's say you're convinced Apple's about to announce something revolutionary (and this time it's actually revolutionary, not just moving the camera to a different corner). You expect the stock to jump over the next month.

But here's the problem: buying 100 shares of Apple would cost you $18,838. That's a lot of money to risk on a hunch, even if you're pretty confident.

Instead, you decide to buy a call option. Here's how that works...

Option Details:

◇ Current Apple price: $188.38

◇ Strike price you choose: $190 (slightly above current price)

◇ Premium (the fee you pay): $5 per share

◇ Contract size: 100 shares (this is standard for all options)

So your total cost is $5 × 100 = $500. Compare that to the $18,838 you'd need to buy the stock outright.

What Happens Next?

Outcome 1: Apple soars to $210

Your call option gives you the right to buy Apple at $190, even though it's now trading at $210.

Your gross profit: ($210 - $190) × 100 = $2,000.

Your net profit: $2,000 - $500 (premium paid) = $1,500

You just turned $500 into $1,500. That's a 300% return.

Outcome 2: Apple disappoints and falls to $185.

Notice the break-even point here: $190 (strike price) + $5 (premium) = $195. The stock needs to rise above $195 for you to profit.

Example 2: Put options on Tesla Inc. (TSLA)

Now let's flip the script. It's April 7, 2025, and Tesla is trading at $239.43. You're convinced Elon's latest Twitter spree is going to tank the stock over the next month.

You buy a put option with these details...

◇ Current Tesla price: $239.43

◇ Strike price: $230

◇ Premium: $7 per share

◇ Total cost: $7 × 100 = $700

◇ Your break-even point: $230 - $7 = $223

What Happens Next?

Outcome 1: Tesla falls to $210. Your put gives you the right to sell Tesla at $230, even though it's only worth $210.

Your gross profit: ($230 - $210) × 100 = $2,000.

Your net profit: $2,000 - $700 = $1,300

Outcome 2: Tesla stays above $230 Your option expires worthless. You lose your $700 premium, but that's your maximum loss.

The Four Basic Options Strategies

Since you can buy or sell both calls and puts, this gives us four basic strategies:

Buying a call: You expect the stock to rise

Selling a call: You expect the stock to stay flat or fall

Buying a put: You expect the stock to fall

Selling a put: You expect the stock to stay flat or rise

From these four building blocks, traders have created hundreds of complex strategies with exotic names like Christmas Tree Spreads, Iron Condors, and Broken Wing Butterflies. (I'm not making these up.)

The Key Difference That Changes Everything

Here's the crucial insight that most people miss...

When you **buy** options, money flows **away** from you (you pay premiums)

When you **sell** options, money flows **to** you (you receive premiums)

A Brief History (Because Context Matters)

Options aren't some newfangled invention. Farmers have used them for centuries to protect against price swings. During the Dutch Tulip Mania in the 1600s, traders used options to speculate on tulip prices (and we all know how that ended).

The real game-changer came in 1973 with the formation of the Chicago Board Options Exchange (CBOE). For the first time, there was a standardized, regulated marketplace for stock options. No more relying on handshake deals or hoping the other party would honor their commitment.

Today, US exchanges handle over $26 billion in daily options volume. That's a lot of activity, and it happens for three main reasons:

1. **Speculation:** This is where options get their bad reputation. New traders treat their apps like casinos, hoping to turn $100 into $10,000 overnight. Most lose everything. We're not doing this.

2. **Hedging:** This is options' original purpose. If you own $100,000 worth of Tesla stock and Elon's tweets keep you awake at night, you can buy $1,000 worth of put options as insurance. Smart money.

3. **Income Generation:** This is our focus. We're using options to create steady cash flow with minimal risk. No gambling, no get-rich-quick schemes, just consistent income.

Now, before moving ahead, let's get ourselves familiarized with some basic options terminology.

Options terminology you are going to encounter throughout this book

◇ **Call options:** Options that give you rights (with no obligations) to buy an asset at a set price before the expiration date.

◇ **Put options:** Options that give you rights (with no obligations) to sell an asset at a set price before the expiration date.

◇ **Strike price:** The price at which you, as an option holder, have the right to buy or sell an asset.

◇ **Premium:** The price you pay to buy options.

◇ **Expiration date:** The date by which you need to exercise the right to buy or sell the underlying asset.

◇ **Days to Expiry (DTE):** It refers to the number of calendar days remaining until the expiration date. We will discuss later how DTE significantly affects the value of an option.

◇ **In the Money (ITM):** In the case of call options, ITM occurs when the price of a stock goes above the strike price. In the case of puts, ITM happens when the stock price falls below the strike price.

◇ **Out of the Money (OTM):** In the case of call options, OTM occurs when the price of a stock falls below the strike price. In the case of puts, OTM happens when the stock rises above the strike price. When an option expires OTM, the value of the option becomes zero.

◇ **At the Money (ATM):** An option is considered ATM when the stock price is equal to, or very close to, the strike price. This applies to both call and put options.

◇ **Options chain**: This is a table that shows all the available options for a stock, with different strike prices and expiries. You can access the options chain of a stock using your trading platform or financial websites like Yahoo Finance.

In addition to these basic terms, there are many more options-related concepts and terminologies. We will discuss their meaning as and when we encounter them in the next chapters.

Final words: why options don't deserve their risky reputations

Unfortunately most retirement and wealth-building books avoid options entirely.

You've probably heard horror stories of people losing their shirts trading options.

But here's the thing... don't blame the tool because some people misuse it.

A hammer can build a house or break a window. The tool isn't the problem; it's how you use it.

The cash-secured put (CSP) strategy we'll focus on generates income with the mindset of a long-term value investor, not a short-term speculator. If speculation is the "dark side" of options, CSPs are the "good side."

So how do they work?

Key takeaways

◇ Options let you lock in a price to buy or sell a stock later. You don't need to own a particular stock to buy/sell options on that stock.

◇ Call options give you the right to buy a stock at a set price before expiry. They are useful when you think a stock will go up.

◇ Puts are useful when you think a stock will go down. Put options give you the rights, without obligations, to sell a stock at a set price before an expiry date.

◇ Expiration is the deadline for an options contract. If you don't use the option by then, it becomes worthless.

◇ You need to pay a premium to buy an option. That's your upfront cost. It's also the maximum amount that you can potentially lose while buying options.

◇ Options can be used for speculation, risk management, and to generate regular income. This book focuses on the third one.

Chapter 3

CASH SECURED PUTS... THE "INSURANCE COMPANY" STRATEGY

"Amateurs want to be right. Professionals want to make money."
- **Alan Abelson**.

L et me ask you something: Do you have insurance?

Of course you do. Car insurance, home insurance, maybe life insurance. You're not alone... over 170 million Americans have some form of life insurance. We buy insurance to protect against disasters, house fires, car accidents, massive medical bills, or worse.

When tragedy strikes, insurance companies are legally obligated to pay out... sometimes millions of dollars. Yet companies like UnitedHealth still manage to generate over $400 billion in annual revenue. How is that possible?

It's simple, they've figured out how to make collecting premiums more profitable than paying out claims.

Here's what they know that most people don't. Adverse events are rare, and with the right calculations, you can collect enough in premiums to cover your risks and still profit handsomely.

Now, what if I told you that you could flip the script? Instead of paying insurance premiums, you could be the one collecting them?

That's exactly what we're going to do with CSPs. You're about to become the insurance company.

What Are Cash Secured Puts (And Why Should You Care)?

Remember from Chapter 2: a put option gives someone the right to sell a stock at a preset price before expiration. When someone buys a put, they're essentially buying insurance against their stock dropping in value.

But here's the key insight: for every put buyer, there's a put seller. And the seller? They collect the premium.

With CSPs, we're going to:

1. Sell put options on stocks we actually want to own
2. Set aside enough cash to buy those shares if we have to
3. Collect premium income while we wait

If this sounds confusing, let me break it down with a real example that'll make everything crystal clear.

The CSP Strategy in Action: A Real Example with Nvidia

Let's break down the entire process into a few steps:

1. **Choosing a stock:** Let's say you have a positive view about Nvidia. You think the stock can be a great long-term asset in your portfolio because of growing AI adoption. (**Note:** Later in the book, we will discuss in more detail how to choose the right stock for CSPs.)

2. **Choosing the right option contract:** Now, if you look at the option chain of Nvidia (you can easily find it on your trading app or financial platforms like Yahoo Finance), you will see call and put options of different expiry dates and strike prices, like this:

May 9, 2025													
May 9	12.12	-6.73 ▼	12.00	12.75	77	499	95.00	2.60	+1.41 ▲	2.50	2.56	1650	4166
May 9	10.05	-7.85 ▼	11.00	11.65	20	238	95.02	2.80	+1.50 ▲	2.76	2.81	416	807
May 9	10.35	-6.46 ▼	10.70	10.95	69	271	97.00	3.10	+1.66 ▲	3.00	3.10	371	737
May 9	9.00	-7.50 ▼	9.60	10.20	69	376	98.00	3.35	+1.72 ▲	3.25	3.40	503	784
May 9	8.85	-6.45 ▼	9.30	9.50	249	282	98.50	3.65	+1.90 ▲	3.55	3.70	386	1074
May 9	8.45	-6.25 ▼	8.65	8.80	1764	1076	100.00	3.94	+1.98 ▲	3.90	4.00	11822	2242
May 9	8.05	-5.90 ▼	8.00	8.15	330	418	101.00	4.70	+2.55 ▲	4.25	4.35	1904	953
May 9	7.45	-5.55 ▼	7.40	7.55	815	430	102.00	5.04	+2.86 ▲	4.60	4.75	1898	1690
May 9	6.80	-5.48 ▼	6.80	6.95	846	486	103.00	5.23	+2.60 ▲	5.00	5.15	564	748
May 9	6.35	-5.00 ▼	6.25	6.35	1146	355	104.00	5.49	+2.67 ▲	5.45	5.55	882	843
May 9	5.80	-4.82 ▼	5.70	5.80	2859	1620	105.00	5.90	+2.80 ▲	5.90	6.00	1585	6416
May 9	5.30	-4.70 ▼	5.20	5.30	1953	652	106.00	6.47	+3.02 ▲	6.35	6.50	353	402
May 9	4.72	-4.78 ▼	4.70	4.80	1134	524	107.00	7.95	+4.29 ▲	6.85	7.00	135	743
May 9	4.10	-4.55 ▼	4.25	4.35	813	861	108.00	7.70	+3.70 ▲	7.40	7.55	253	1071
May 9	3.61	-4.24 ▼	3.80	3.90	483	691	109.00	10.40	+6.05 ▲	7.95	8.15	171	804
May 9	3.45	-3.95 ▼	3.40	3.50	3484	3368	110.00	9.20	+4.54 ▲	8.55	9.05	501	5581
May 9	3.10	-3.60 ▼	3.05	3.15	525	928	111.00	9.93	+4.78 ▲	8.85	9.75	52	1201
May 9	2.65	-3.40 ▼	2.70	2.78	1565	1730	112.00	11.52	+5.92 ▲	9.85	10.05	186	682
May 9	2.36	-3.19 ▼	2.39	2.46	716	1229	113.00	12.39	+8.29 ▲	10.50	10.75	2161	2219
May 9	2.00	-3.04 ▼	2.11	2.18	888	1410	114.00	13.60	+6.82 ▲	11.25	11.45	43	277

Figure 4: NVIDIA option chain (Source: NASDAQ)

Let's say on April 17, 2025, Nvidia is trading at $104.49. We are going to choose the put option with the following details:

◇ **Strike price**: $100

◇ **Expiry date**: May 9, 2025

◇ **Value of the put option**: $3.94

Now, you may be wondering how to choose the right put option from so many alternatives. Let's not get overwhelmed with every concept in a single chapter. We will delve into all these in later chapters. For now, let's keep things simple and understand how CSPs work.

3. **Sell the put option and secure it with cash:** Since you might have to buy 100 shares of Nvidia at your strike price ($100), you set aside $10,000. But since you collect $394 in premium for selling the put option, you only need to tie up $9,606 of your own money. This will be returned to you when the contract finishes.

4. **Wait and win**: Now you're in a win-win situation.

Scenario 1: Nvidia finishes above $100 on May 9th (known as finishing Out of The Money - OTM)

If your CSP expires OTM, the option expires worthless. You keep the entire $394 premium. That's a 4.1% return in less than a month ($394 ÷ $9,606), which annualizes to roughly 50%. You can now repeat the strategy next month.

Scenario 2: Nvidia finishes below $100 on May 9th (known as finishing In The Money - ITM)

If your CSP expires ITM, you get "assigned" meaning you have to buy 100 shares at $100 each. But remember, you collected $3.94 per share in premium, so your effective purchase price is $96.06. You just bought a stock you wanted at a 8% discount to where it was trading when you started!

The Beautiful Truth About CSPs

This is why CSPs are often called a hybrid strategy, because you get...

◇ Regular income when options expire worthless
◇ Value investing opportunities when you get assigned quality stocks at discounted prices

It's like being paid to place limit orders on stocks you want to own.

CSPs vs. Naked Puts - Swimming With vs. Without a Life Vest

Before we go further, let me warn you about something you should never do, which is selling "naked" puts.

A naked put is when you sell put options without having the cash to buy the stock if assigned. It's like swimming in the ocean without a life vest... sure, you might be fine, but if something goes wrong, you're in serious trouble.

Here's what happens with naked puts. Let's say you sell that same Nvidia put but only have $2,000 in your account instead of the full $10,000. If Nvidia crashes and you get assigned, your broker will issue a margin call demanding you deposit more money immediately. If you can't, they'll liquidate your positions at the worst possible time, locking in massive losses.

CSPs are the complete opposite. You're swimming with a life vest. You have the cash ready, so you sleep peacefully regardless of what the market does.

Why CSPs Are Actually Conservative (Yes, Really)

I know what you're thinking: "Options? Conservative? You've got to be kidding."

But here are the facts: According to data from The Motley Fool, the S&P 500 delivered positive monthly returns 59% of the time over the past 96 years. Most of the remaining months were flat or only slightly negative.

This means CSPs work in your favor the majority of the time. In neutral or rising markets, the puts you sell expire worthless and you keep all the premium. Even in slightly declining markets, you often still profit.

Plus, time is on your side. As expiration approaches, options lose value due to time decay. This means you can profit even when stocks go nowhere.

The Three Pillars of CSP Success

For CSPs to work their magic, you only need three things…

◇ Cash backing: You have the money to buy the stock if assigned

◇ Quality stocks: You only sell puts on companies you'd genuinely want to own

◇ Neutral to bullish outlook: You believe the stock will at least hold steady or rise

When these three elements align, CSPs become one of the most reliable income strategies in the market.

Your Next Step

In the coming chapters, we'll dive deep into exactly how to choose the right stocks, pick the optimal strike prices and expiration dates, and manage your positions for maximum profit.

Key takeaways

◇ Using CSP, you can play the role of an insurance company. Here, you can collect premiums just like insurers do, but with calculated risk.

◇ You only sell CSPs on stocks you want to own. This means even if an assignment happens, you end up buying the stock you already like, and that too at a better price.

◇ CSP can give you surprisingly high returns with limited risks, as even modest monthly premiums can add up.

◇ Unlike naked puts, CSP is backed by cash, not margin. So, you never have to borrow money to cover your position.

◇ CSP works best in neutral and bullish markets. In these markets, most options expire worthless, and time decay works in your favor.

Chapter 4

THE BILLION-DOLLAR SECRET WARREN BUFFETT DOESN'T WANT YOU TO KNOW

"Do more of what works and less of what doesn't."
– Steve Clark

When you hear "Warren Buffett," what comes to mind? Probably a wise old man in Omaha preaching about the magic of compounding, right? Maybe you picture him sipping Cherry Coke while dispensing folksy wisdom about buying great companies and holding them forever. The media loves to paint him as the ultimate buy-and-hold investor who wouldn't touch anything as "risky" as options.

But here's what they don't tell you...

Between 2004 and 2008, while everyone was calling him the "Oracle of Omaha" and the "champion of value investing," Buffett was quietly making billions from options. Specifically, he was selling put options on major stock indexes like the S&P 500, FTSE 100, Euro Stoxx 50, and Nikkei 225.

His strategy was beautifully simple: He had a long-term bullish view on stocks in general (shocking, I know), so he sold European-style put options on these indexes. These are special puts that can only be exercised at expiration, unlike the American-style options we'll be using, which can be exercised anytime.

Buffett's reasoning was straightforward: "In the long run, stocks tend to perform well, and these indexes will rise, making these options worthless."

The result? Nearly $5 billion in premium income.

In his 2008 letter to shareholders, Buffett wrote with characteristic understatement:

> *"We have received premiums of $4.9 billion, money we have invested. We, meanwhile, have paid nothing, since all expiration dates are far in the future."*

Let that sink in for a moment. The world's most famous value investor... the guy who supposedly never speculates... the man who calls derivatives "financial weapons of mass destruction"... quietly collected $5 billion selling options.

The Hypocrisy (Or Is It Genius?)

Now, you might be thinking, "Wait a minute. Didn't Buffett also call derivatives dangerous?"

He did. But here's the key distinction: Buffett wasn't speculating or gambling. He was using options the same way we're going to use Cash Secured Puts (CSPs)... as a conservative income strategy backed by solid fundamentals and plenty of cash.

The difference between Buffett's approach and the options horror stories you hear about is simple: preparation and purpose.

Buffett had the cash to back his positions. He chose quality underlying assets. He had a long-term view. And most importantly, he was getting paid to do something he wanted to do anyway (invest in broad market indexes).

Sound familiar? That's exactly what we covered in the previous chapter about CSPs.

Why This Matters to You

If options are good enough for the world's greatest investor to generate billions in income, maybe... just maybe... they're worth considering for your portfolio too.

The truth is, many of your investing role models use options to amplify returns. They just don't talk about it much because it doesn't fit the narrative the financial media wants to tell.

But you're not here for narratives. You're here for results.

In the previous chapter, we covered the basic mechanics of CSPs. Now let's dive deeper into the full range of benefits this strategy offers... and why it might be the missing piece in your retirement income puzzle.

Benefit 1: Generating consistent income

In chapter 3, we took Nvidia's example to show how you can generate regular premium income using CSPs. Now, let's take another blue-chip stock to explore how income generated from CSPs can beat dividend investing or even simple buy-and-hold investing by miles:

On April 17, 2025, Microsoft is trading at $373. We are going to choose the following put option:

Strike price: $340 (around 9% out of the money (OTM)).

Expiry date: May 9, 2025

Option price: $5.45

So, the total premium you get by entering into the position is $5.45 * 100 = $545.

Your total cash requirement = (Strike price * 100) - Total premium received = ($340 * 100) - $545 = $34,000 - $545 = $33,455.

Monthly return = $545/$33,455 * 100 = 0.0163 * 100 = 1.63%.

Now, if you keep repeating the strategy every month, CSPs give you about 20% in annualized return. Compare that with Microsoft's current dividend yield of about 0.89%: the CSP strategy beats Microsoft's dividend yield by more than 20 times! But that's not the only way CSPs help you beat dividend investing or the buy-and-hold strategy. Let's look at what happens when a drawdown happens:

Suppose you are buying Microsoft at the current market price of $373. Now, let's say the trade war worsens and Microsoft tanks to $300. If you are buying and holding, you are going to experience a drawdown of more than 19%.

Here are the calculations:

Drawdown = ($373 - $300)/$373 * 100 = $73/$373 * 100 = 0.1957 * 100 = **19.57%.**

Let's see what happens when you are using the CSP:

Under the CSP strategy, you get to buy Microsoft stock at $340. And, if we deduct the premium, your effective buying price becomes $340 - $5.45 = $334.55.

So, you are going to experience a drawdown of ($334.55 - $300)/$334.55 * 100 = $34.55/$334.55 * 100 = 0.1033 * 100 = 10.33%

The CSP strategy cuts your maximum drawdown by around half!

But wait, there is more to it. Let's look at how you can take a portfolio approach and carry out CSPs on multiple stocks to target better returns, stagger cashflows across weeks, and spread your risk.

Scaling income with multiple positions

Let's assume you are bullish on these 3 stocks: Apple (AAPL), JPMorgan Chase (JPM), and Procter & Gamble (PG). Here are the details of the put options we are going to choose to carry out the CSP strategy with a portfolio approach:

1. **AAPL**

   Current price: $196.98

   Price of the May 16, $180 strike put option: $3.70

   Total premium income = $3.70 * 100 = $370.

   Total cash required = (Strike price * 100) - Total premium = ($180 * 100) - $370 = $18,000 - $370 = $17,630.

2. **JPM**

   Current price: $231.96

   Price of the May 16, $210 strike put option: $2.05

   Total premium income = $2.05 * 100 = $205.

   Total cash required = (Strike price * 100) - Total premium = ($210 * 100) - $205 = $21,000 - $205 = $20,795.

3. **PG**

   Current price: $170.63

   Price of the May 16, $155 strike put option: $0.98

   Total premium income = $0.98 * 100 = $98.

   Total cash required = (Strike price * 100) - Total premium = ($155 * 100) - $98 = $15,500 - $98 = $15,402.

Now, let's calculate the total premium income and the total cash deployed in all three positions:

Total income from premiums = $370 + $205 + $98 = $673.

Total cash deployed = $17,630 + $20,795 + $15,402 = $53,827.

Total return = $673/ $53,827 * 100 = 0.0125 * 100 = 1.25%/month.

So, the combined position gives you an annualized return of about 15% by deploying $53,827.

Note that we chose the same expiration date (May 16, 2025) for all three positions here. However, you can stagger the expiry dates (for instance, choosing the May 16 put for AAPL and the May 23 put for JPM) to generate weekly income flow.

You can keep reinvesting your premiums to earn even more by compounding your income. Look at the following table showing how compounding your monthly CSP earnings can exponentially grow your capital (let's assume that you started with $10,000):

Weekly return	Monthly return	1 year	2 years	3 years	3-year total return
0.25%	1.09%	$11,390	$12,970	$14,760	48%
0.5%	2.18%	$12,960	$16,800	$21,770	118%
1%	4.41%	$16,780	$28,150	$47,220	372%

Table 2: Exponential growth of capital through CSPs

The portfolio approach helps you diversify risks across multiple stocks. So if one position takes an unexpected hit, you have other stocks to balance out returns. Moreover, your income CSPs can supplement your traditional retirement income sources, like social security, annuities, or high-yield savings accounts. This takes us to the next point.

Retirement account application

Currently, an average retired worker in the US receives $1,920 a month in social security benefits. However, an average retired household spends in the neighbourhood of $5,000 per month. This leaves you with an income gap of more than $3,000. It's hard to bridge that gap without nibbling into your savings.

This is where CSPs can fit in, especially when you use CSPs within a retirement account like a Traditional or Roth IRA. These accounts offer tax-deferred or tax-free growth of your capital. As you saw earlier in the chapter, with a low to moderate risk approach, you can generate

1.5-2% per month by applying CSPs on blue-chip stocks like Microsoft, Apple, Nvidia, Alphabet, or Amazon.

1.5–2% per month translates into $1,500 to $2,000 in monthly income from a $100,000 account. This extra income can bridge the larger area of your retirement income gap. And because it's inside an IRA, you don't need to worry about taxation until you start withdrawing (or not tax worries at all in the case of a Roth IRA).

Benefit 2: Acquiring stocks at a discount

Example 1: Building a position in growth stocks

How often does it happen that you have spotted a great stock, but you feel the current price is a little too high to enter? You probably add such stocks to your watch list and keep monitoring them for a dip, while your money sits idle in your brokerage account (or earning peanuts in savings accounts). CSPs help you earn 20-30% in annualized income while you are waiting for your favourite stock to give you a great entry point. In chapter 4, we discussed this in brief. Let's take a real-life example to understand how to get strategic entry points using CSPs:

Suppose Nvidia is currently trading at $100, and you feel the stock is a bit expensive at this price. You think that a 10% correction in the stock will give you enough margin of safety. Here is how you can apply the CSP to create the possibility of such a lower entry point.

You can choose a $90-strike put option to expire in 30 days (let's assume it's selling at $3.5).

So, selling the put option helps you earn $350 ($3.5*100) in premium. And if the stock price falls and the option is exercised, you get to buy Nvidia for $90. In fact, the premium of $3.5 makes your effective entry price $90-$3.5 = $86.5. The lower effective price gives you some extra cushion to absorb market pullback, as we discussed in the Microsoft example above.

You may be thinking, "We could buy a stock at the price we want using limit orders as well, so what's special about CSPs?" Well, while you place a limit order to buy a stock at a defined price, your money gets locked in your brokerage account, and it doesn't earn any interest. The CSP strategy, on the other hand, helps you earn premiums while you wait for the stock price to come down. That's the difference between your money doing nothing vs. earning 20-30% in annualized income. Which one would you take?

Example 2: Market correction opportunity

Are we allowed to use the phrase "value investing on steroids" because value investing is not commonly associated with anything fast or aggressive? But when you layer value investing with CSPs, it feels quite like injecting growth hormone into the slow-growing muscles of value investing.

One of the fundamental rules of value investing is to find stocks selling below what they are truly worth (or their intrinsic value). Howard Marks, whose company Oaktree Capital Management manages assets of over $200 billion, defines value investing as

"Figuring out what something's worth and seeing if you can buy it at or below that price."

CSPs can precisely help you do that: buying a stock at a substantially low price, especially during market corrections. Let's take an example to understand how it works:

During the 2022 market pullback, Costco (COST) declined from a high of $600.04 on April 8, 2022, to a low of $416.43 on May 20, 2022. That's more than a 30% drop in six weeks. Let's assume that when the stock fell significantly, and was trading at around $450, you decided to sell the $420 strike put. Since the volatility was high, the options prices were higher than usual, too. (Note: In Chapter 10, we will discuss how higher volatility leads to higher options prices, benefiting you as an options seller.). So, let's say you received $12 as a premium by selling the $400 put. Your total premium income was $12 * 100 = $1,200.

Since the stock price eventually fell below the strike price, you would have been assigned the stock. After deducting the premiums, your effective purchase price would be $420 - $12 = $408.

The correction was short-lived, and Costco soon rebounded. By mid-August, you could exit the stock at around $550 with about a 26% gain. Or had you been holding the stock till today (April 2025), when the stock is trading at $1,000, you would have pocketed over 145% in net returns in less than 3 years! That's value investing on steroids, we were just talking about.

As we can see in the Costco example, you can strategically use CSPs during market declines to accumulate great stocks at even greater prices. You can create a market watchlist during such pullbacks and start selling CSPs on the stocks showing the best potential returns. And if you are thinking, "If the market continues to decline, how do CSPs help me?", here is the answer:

The premium income gives you a cushion by lowering your effective cost basis. So, the maximum drawdown you experience is generally lower than buying the stock outright in a declining market. Moreover, as we have said before, you should be applying the CSP strategy only to stocks with great fundamentals. So, even if they decline beyond what you expected, they are more likely to bounce back strong during recovery.

Benefit 3: Enhancing your overall portfolio returns

Like all investing strategies, CSPs, too, should not be carried out in isolation. They need to be a part of your overall portfolio strategy. And, we have evidence to support that CSPs can enhance your overall portfolio returns. Let's look at the example of the classic 60/40 portfolio (60% stocks and 40% bonds):

Backtesting results on a typical 60/40 portfolio consisting of MSCI World stocks (60%) and FTSE World Government Bond - Developed Markets (40%) show that the portfolio generated a 7.6% annualized return in four decades between 1986 and 2024. However, in the previous examples, we saw that it's quite reasonable to conservatively expect 12-15% returns using CSPs alone. Returns that we have achieved in our own portfolios, and many of our students have replicated.

Moreover, as the premium income provides a cushion to your portfolio during drawdowns, including CSPs in your overall investment strategy can lower your maximum drawdown while boosting your portfolio returns.

More importantly, you don't need to completely overhaul your existing portfolio to include CSPs. You can start by lowering your bond exposure and using the capital to apply CSPs to 1 or 2 stocks. As your capital grows with regular income, you can take a portfolio approach to apply CSPs on multiple stocks (preferably 3 to 5 stocks). We think that combining CSPs with long-term holding can optimize the performance of your portfolio.

Benefit 4: Reducing volatility in your investment approach

Imagine the last time you were flying and there was some severe turbulence. What was going on in your mind? Even after knowing that the plane wings are not just going to snap off, we want those episodes to pass as fast as possible. The reason is that the irrational or emotional sides of us want to avoid uncertainties. In investing, volatility appears like turbulence: it's emotionally catastrophic, and you want to avoid it. Past market data shows that CSPs help bring more stability to your portfolio while avoiding those emotional and financial jolts:

The Chicago Board Options Exchange (CBOE) has a financial metric called the "PUT Index". The index tracks the performance of a simple options strategy: selling a put option on the S&P 500 every month. When this strategy is backtested from 1986 to 2024, it has generated a

9.54% annualized return. This is almost the same as the 9.80% from the S&P 500 in the same period. But here is the dramatic difference in the performance between the two indexes: the PUT Index had a standard deviation of 9.95%, while the S&P 500's was a much bumpier 14.93%. Standard deviation in return tells how much the returns of an investment deviate from the average. So, the higher the standard deviation, the higher the volatility.

> **Note:** To get a bit more technical, the PUT Index had a higher Sharpe ratio (0.65 vs 0.49) compared to the S&P 500 in the period. The Sharpe Ratio tells you how much return you get per unit of risk. So, a higher Sharpe ratio means you are earning a higher return for the same risk level.

The key takeaway for you is this: the CSP strategy helps you avoid dramatic market swings to a great extent. Low volatility means you are not compelled to look at your screen every second to monitor your positions or worry about a sharp drop in your portfolio. That also means no emotional decisions, more peace of mind, and better sleep at night. These probably aren't too much to ask for when all you want is to enjoy life before time slips away!

Key takeaways

◇ Instead of sitting on idle cash, CSPs allow you to generate income upfront by selling puts on stocks you already want to own.

◇ CSPs also let you set your own "buy price." If the stock drops, you get to buy your favourite stock cheaper than today's market price while keeping the premium.

◇ Even if the stock never hits your strike price, you pocket the premium. You can keep repeating the strategy to compound returns.

◇ CSPs create a buffer against market swings. This means you're investing with a margin of safety and avoiding the emotional rollercoaster ride.

◇ CSPs help you build a better retirement strategy. It turns cash into income, without relying on low returns from dividends or savings accounts.

◇ CSPs help you lower the volatility of your investing approach.

Chapter 5

THE $30,000 LESSON HE LEARNED SO YOU DON'T HAVE TO

"It's good to learn from your mistakes. It's better to learn from other people's mistakes."
- **Warren Buffett**.

I'll never forget the Discord message I got from Zach in May 2022.

Zach had been one of my most enthusiastic students. Smart guy, successful accountant, methodical in everything he did. He'd been running CSPs for about six months and was absolutely crushing it. Making $3,000-$4,000 a month in premium income like clockwork.

Then the call came.

"Oliver," he said, and I could hear the defeat in his voice. "I screwed up. Bad."

Over the next twenty minutes, Zach and I went back and forth about how he'd gotten greedy. How he'd started chasing higher and higher premiums. How he'd abandoned everything we'd taught him about stock selection and risk management. How he'd ended up with positions in companies he'd never heard of, selling puts way too close to the money on stocks that had no business being in anyone's portfolio.

The final damage? $30,000 wiped out in just 6 weeks.

"I thought I was smarter than the strategy," he admitted. "I thought I could juice the returns just a little bit more."

Zach learned an expensive lesson that day. But here's the thing... you don't have to.

Why We're Doing This Backwards

Most investing books save the "mistakes" chapter for the end, like some afterthought. They spend 200 pages telling you how amazing their strategy is, then casually mention in Chapter 12 that "oh, by the way, here are some things that could go wrong."

That's backwards.

I want you to know what can go wrong before we dive deeper into the technical details. I want you to learn from Zach's $30,000 mistake, and the dozens of other costly errors I've seen students make over the years.

Why? Because once you understand the pitfalls, everything else we cover will make more sense. You'll read the next chapters with a more critical eye. You'll be more mindful when you see those tempting high premiums. You'll think twice before abandoning your position management rules.

The Real Cost of Learning the Hard Way

Here's what most people don't realize: in the options world, mistakes aren't just expensive... they're often catastrophic.

With regular stock investing, if you buy a bad stock, it might go down 20%, 30%, maybe even 50% in a really bad scenario. You lose money, but you still have something left.

With options, especially when you start getting fancy or greedy, you can lose your entire position in a matter of weeks.

Zach was lucky. He lost $30,000, but he still had money left to rebuild. I've talked to others who weren't so fortunate.

The Good News

Here's the thing about CSP mistakes: they're almost all preventable. They're not random market events or acts of God. They're the result of specific, identifiable errors in judgment.

And once you know what to look for, they're easy to avoid.

Over the next few pages, I'm going to walk you through the most common (and costly) mistakes I've seen CSP traders make. Some of these might seem obvious in hindsight. Others might surprise you. All of them have cost real people real money.

But by the time you finish this chapter, you'll be armed with the knowledge to sidestep every one of these traps.

Because as Warren Buffett said, it's better to learn from other people's mistakes. And trust me, I've got plenty of other people's mistakes to share with you.

Let's start with the big one... the mistake that's probably cost more CSP traders more money than all the others combined.

Mistake 1: Chasing high premiums on risky stocks

Which of the following option trades would you take?

	Trade 1: Stock A	Trade 2: Stock B
Current Price (Apr 17)	$195.17	$2.74
Put Option	May 23, Strike $175	May 23, Strike $2.50
Premium	$4.00	$0.17
Out-of-the-Money (OTM)	10.27%	8.76%
Return from Premium	2.29%	6.8%
Annualized Return	26.91%	75.21%

Table 3: *Trade 1 vs. Trade 2*

Of course, the choice is pretty obvious. Anyone without an iota of knowledge about puts or calls can tell you that Trade 2 gives a better deal: a 75.21% annualized return vs. 26.91% return by Trade 1.

But in investing, the easy answer is rarely the correct answer.

Here, stock A is Apple (AAPL), the bluest of the blue-chip stocks. It's a tech giant that just reported $124.3 billion in revenue in the last quarter (Q1, 2025). Apple has delivered over 196% total returns in the previous five years. $1,000 invested in the stock in April 2020 would be worth $2,965.90 today (April 2025).

In comparison, had you invested $1,000 in stock B five years ago, you would be left with little more than $150 today. That wipes out almost 85% of your capital. That's how Stock B, AMC Entertainment (AMC), stands in comparison to Apple (AAPL).

While Trade 2 gives you a much higher potential income from the premium, it's not a stock you would want to own. Note that stocks with high volatility tend to have higher premiums. For instance, AMC has a current implied volatility (IV) of 84.6 in comparison with Apple's much more sober 42.7. This means the market expects AMC to swing wildly, up or down. In comparison, Apple is expected to show more stable price behavior. (**Note:** We will discuss IV in more detail in later chapters.)

However, the CSP strategy is not about chasing high premiums only. While premium income is one leg of the strategy, the other leg is your willingness to own the stock in the long run.

A key mistake that many new traders make in CSPs is chasing high premiums by overlooking the fundamentals of the stock. CSPs should be carried out only on stocks you are confident about and that you would like to own. Here, even though AMC might give you better premiums, you wouldn't like to hold a stock that resembles gambling! Here is the key takeaway: First, create a list of fundamentally strong stocks, and then choose among them to carry out CSPs based on the earning potential of a specific trade. Avoid stocks with high premiums but with fundamentals of a falling knife!

Mistake 2: Ignoring broader market conditions

Imagine this: It's January 2022, and Meta is trading at around $330. You sold the $310 strike put to collect $6 in premium (total premium = $6*100 = $600). But within the first week of February, the stock was trading at below $250. You were assigned the stock, and you told yourself, "I am buying the dip, it's a bargain". However, as the year progressed, the dip kept dipping, and Meta dropped to under $90 by November. It was a nearly 70% decline. The overall market was bleeding as well. The S&P lost about 20% that year. The price of Meta didn't rise above your purchase price until the end of 2023. Your capital was stuck for about 2 years.

What could you do differently?

The answer leads us to the second mistake that many new traders make: ignoring the overall market conditions. Carrying out CSPs seems effortless in a bull market, as happened in 2021. The S&P 500 went up by more than 28.75% that year. Many new traders were aggressively selling puts and comfortably earning premiums without thinking about the downside. The market sentiment changed sharply from the very beginning of 2022. The negative sentiment in the broader market trickled down to large-cap tech stocks like Meta, Nvidia, and Tesla. When there is a major change in market trend, volatility rises, which pushes premiums higher. And these higher premiums are likely to tempt you into taking a trade.

However, when the market sentiment becomes grimmer, individual stocks, as in the case of Meta, can take a big hit. So, when assignments happen, you may be forced to hold stock for a very long period. However, judging the market conditions can help you make more informed decisions. For instance, in Meta's case, as the market sentiment was negative, you could have chosen a lower strike price (that could lower your max drawdown). You could also wait for the market to stabilize before entering into a trade. Moreover, you could pick a different stock or sector, as the tech sector was taking the maximum beating.

Ignoring the broader market conditions can place you in a situation you didn't expect (like the emotional pain of seeing your holdings losing value every day). So, look at the overall market and decide if you are comfortable trading under these dynamics. If not, wait for the market to stabilize.

There will always be a better day to trade!

Mistake 3: Overtrading and commission drag

If there is a list of the gravest sins in any type of trading, from options and stocks to crypto, overtrading would probably top the list. If you have heard that 80-90% of new traders lose money in trading, you can put the blame on a single cause: overtrading.

When you're new to the market, it's very tempting to get caught up in the excitement of making some quick bucks. **However, excitement is probably the most overused and least necessary emotion in trading or investing.**

As economist Paul Samuelson said...

> *"Investing should be more like watching paint dry or watching grass grow. If you want excitement, take $800 and go to Las Vegas."*

When you are jumping in and out of trades, you're probably not spending enough time selecting the right stocks, calculating risks vs. rewards, judging the market conditions, or looking at the technical aspects.

Overtrading also means you are taking an ultra-short-term view of the market and expecting to get your trades right immediately. That's not the right expectation.

Your entries should be well-calculated so that you won't have to prematurely close a trade at the first sign of the market moving in the "wrong" direction. Even though there is no rule of thumb regarding how frequently you should trade, data shows that the more frequently you trade, the worse your trading results can be.

Additionally, overtrading is bound to lower your returns because of something called "commission drag".

Every time you place a trade, your broker is going to charge a commission. Leading US brokers like Interactive Brokers, Fidelity, and Charles Schwab charge $0.65 per contract. So, each time you open a position with 1 contract and then close it, you need to pay $1.30 as commission. Now add Exchange and Regulatory Fees on top of that commission, and your round trip costs you around $1.40. That may sound like a small fee, but when you trade frequently and use multiple contracts, these small fees can easily add up and drag your total returns. For instance, if you trade 25 contracts per week, that's $35+ in fees per week, or more than $1,800 a year. While in recent years trading commissions have come down significantly across brokers, it's still important to watch out for the small costs.

Mistake 4: Psychological pitfalls of options trading

We are human beings, deeply flawed emotional creatures. We feel excited about new things, and we get scared of the unknown. The prospect of easy money often makes us exhilarated, which can easily shroud our judgment. Or when we are scared to the core of an imminent danger, we take desperate decisions. Think of some of your life decisions you aren't proud of. What were you thinking back then? It was probably an emotionally charged moment that pushed you to make a not-so-well-thought-out decision.

Researchers say that our emotions, like fear, anger, frustration, or even sadness, have survival value. These emotions help us avoid dangers and protect ourselves. For instance, the fight-or-flight response helps you run when you are face-to-face with a wild lion in the wilderness of Kenya. In such moments, you need to run for your life. But trading is not one such moment. Here, your anger, frustration, emotional setback, or the fight or flight response aren't going to help you survive.

In fact, a key reason behind trading errors or overtrading is our emotional response. Think of this: you entered into a trade with a particular view of the market. However, soon the price starts moving in the opposite direction. You get scared, and you exit the trade. However, this was just a slight pullback, and the price again starts moving in the direction you initially anticipated. Oh, you just missed a great trade!

You are excited again, and you open a new position. How often has that happened to you? The main reason behind such behavior is our emotional reaction to the market moves. So, what can you do about it? First, be aware of your emotional state. Are you taking this trade because your previous trade ended in a loss, and you want to recover your loss? Stop, you're probably revenge trading.

Second, keep your emotions away from trading decisions. It's very difficult to be completely unemotional, especially when real money is involved. But you need to keep a check on your emotions as much as you can while you are making a trading decision. So, here is a key takeaway... for the right trades, it's not only important to have a stable market but also a stable emotional state.

Conclusion

We all want to make the right decisions without making any mistakes, ever. That sounds like a good wish. But it's not practical. We learn to become good traders or investors by doing the hard thing every day and by accumulating small learnings over time. Some mistakes will always creep in. The trick is to keep the mistakes small, correct them fast, and survive to trade again tomorrow.

Trading is not an all-or-nothing business. You get better at it by taking an iterative approach, by reviewing what worked and what didn't. Moreover, it's always a good idea to avoid mistakes by learning from others. Because not all lessons need to be learned the hard way. As Warren Buffett said, "It is good to learn from your mistakes. It is better to learn from other people's mistakes."

Now that you know the basics of CSPs and what can potentially go wrong, the action is going to be more real now. We will teach you how to execute your first CSP. Let's begin with choosing the right broker first.

Key takeaways

◇ Many new traders often chase high premiums by overlooking the fundamentals of the stock. However, CSPs should be carried out only on stocks you are confident about and that you would like to own.

◇ Look at the overall market conditions before entering into a trade. The broader market can have an immense effect on individual stocks and the performance of your trade.

◇ Overtrading leads to bad trades, trading mistakes, and commission drag. Lower the frequency of your trades. Choose quality over quantity.

◇ Keep your emotions away from your trading decisions. Emotional decisions are the main cause behind overtrading or revenge trading.

Chapter 6

THE $680 HIDDEN TAX YOUR "FREE" BROKER IS CHARGING YOU

"Beware of little expenses. A small leak will sink a great ship."
- Benjamin Franklin.

Quick question: When I say "low-cost broker," what's the first name that pops into your head?

If you just perked up like Hermione Granger and shouted "Robinhood!" you're not alone. Over the past few years, Robinhood has become synonymous with "commission-free trading" and "beginner-friendly investing."

But here's the thing about "free"... it's usually anything but.

The $680 Surprise

Remember my student Zach from the last chapter? The one who lost $30,000? Well, before that disaster, he made another costly mistake that flew completely under his radar.

Zach was using Robinhood for his CSP trades. He figured, "Hey, zero commissions means more profit for me, right?"

Wrong.

After six months of trading, Zach decided to do some math. He'd made about $18,000 in premium income, which should have been fantastic. But when he compared his order fill prices to the actual mid-market prices, he discovered something shocking.

He was losing an average of $6.80 for every $100 he traded.

On his $10,000 in monthly trading volume, that meant Robinhood was quietly skimming $680 every single month from his profits. Over six months, that "free" broker had cost him over $4,000 in hidden fees.

The Dirty Secret of "Commission-Free" Trading

This isn't just Zach's story. According to a 2024 study by finance professors at UC Irvine and Washington University in St. Louis, Robinhood users face an average of $6.80 in transaction costs for every $100 traded.

That's a nearly 7% hidden tax on every trade.

"But wait," you might be thinking, "Robinhood says zero commissions right there on their website!"

They're not lying. You won't see a commission charge on your statement. But what they don't advertise is how they make their money: by selling your order flow to market makers who give you worse prices than you could get elsewhere.

It's like going to a "free" restaurant where they don't charge you for the meal, but they water down your drink, give you smaller portions, and pocket the difference. Technically free, but you're getting less value.

Why This Matters More for Options Traders

If you're just buying and holding index funds, these execution differences might not matter much. A few cents here and there won't make or break your retirement.

But when you're running CSPs with even a moderate size account, you're making multiple trades per week. You're dealing with bid-ask spreads and you're trying to squeeze every bit of profit out of premium collection.

Those "few cents" add up fast.

Let's say you're generating $2,000 per month in premium income (a reasonable target with a $50,000 account). If your broker is skimming 7% through poor execution, that's $140 per month... $1,680 per year... gone.

Over a decade? That's nearly $17,000 in lost profits.

The Real Cost of "Cheap"

But poor execution isn't the only hidden cost of discount brokers. There's also:

Customer service nightmares: Try calling a discount broker when you have an urgent options question. Good luck getting a human.

Platform limitations: Many discount brokers have clunky options interfaces that make complex strategies difficult to execute.

Account restrictions: Some brokers limit your options trading level or require higher account minimums for certain strategies.

The Good News

Here's the thing, you can absolutely run CSPs with any broker, including the one you might already have. The strategy works regardless.

But your experience and profitability will vary dramatically depending on which broker you choose.

You don't want to see a big chunk of your trading profits eaten up by hidden costs. And when you need help troubleshooting a trade, you probably don't want to chat with a bot giving you canned responses.

Key features to look for in an options broker

1. Quality of execution

After you place a buy/sell order through your broker's trading platform, your order is sent for execution. The quality of the execution, however, depends on how the order is fulfilled, how fast, and at what price. Some brokers, for instance, Robinhood, E-Trade, and Webull, use an order fulfillment method called "Payment for Order Flow (PFOF)". In this model, a broker routes the orders to the market maker offering the highest commission rather than the one providing the best execution price.

Because of this PFOF method, you may end up incurring high transaction costs with brokers like Robinhood, even though they charge no upfront fees! For instance, suppose you are selling a put option and the market is bidding $2.00 for it. If your broker executes well, you are supposed to get $2 for it. However, if the order gets fulfilled for $1.95, you just lost $5 ($0.05 * 100) per contract! If you trade 10 contracts, that's $50 gone simply because of bad execution by your broker.

Then there are brokers like Interactive Brokers, which ensure that trades are executed at the best available prices without compromise. These brokers actively seek the best execution price across multiple exchanges. Sticking to brokers with great execution can help you save thousands of dollars in the long run. So, keep an eye on the execution performance published by your broker.

2. Commission and fees

Commissions and fees constitute the most visible part of your trading costs. When you are executing CSPs, there are broadly three types of commissions/fees to be paid:

Per-trade or per-contract commission charged by your broker for opening or closing positions

It's now increasingly common for brokers to charge a per-contract commission (ranging between $0.5 and $1) for opening or closing positions. For instance, Charles Schwab, Fidelity, Interactive Brokers, and E*Trade charge $0.65 per contract, both to open and close. This means when you place an order to sell 2 contracts of a put option, you need to pay $1.30 as commission. Similarly, you pay $1.30 again when you close the position. So, the round-trip costs you $2.60.

Some options-focused brokers, for instance, Tastytrade, have a capped commission structure. Tastytrade charges $1.00 per contract to open a position and $0 to close. The total commission is capped at a maximum of $10 per leg. So, if you are selling 2 contracts of a put option, you'll pay $2.00 to open the trade. But when you close the position, you pay nothing. So your total round-trip commission is just $2.00. And if you are trading 15 or 20 contracts, you pay a maximum of $10 as commission because of the cap.

The assignment fees you pay when stocks are assigned to you

Some brokers may charge you between $5 to $15 every time the option buyer exercises the option and you are assigned the stocks. However, higher competition in the brokerage space has forced many brokers to completely do away with these fees. For instance, Fidelity, Charles Schwab, and Interactive Brokers now charge no fees for assignment. Tastytrade charges a flat $5 fee for an assignment. On the higher side, TradeStation charges $14.95 for an assignment.

Fees charged by government regulators

These fees constitute the smallest component of all types of fees and commissions related to trading options. In the US, some of the government and regulatory fees for options include the Options Regulatory Fee (ORF), the SEC fee, and the FINRA Trading Activity Fee (TAF). Together, they probably add up to just a few cents per options contract (typically between $0.02 and $0.06 per contract). These fees go to the respective government agency or regulatory body to keep the securities market functioning.

3. Specialty of the broker

Not all brokers are designed to serve every customer in the same way. And, it's actually good for you. The requirements of a long-term investor are totally different from someone who sells CSPs every week. A long-term investor is hardly ever looking at the daily charts or the trend lines. They are more interested in financial data like earnings reports and dividends.

But when you are dealing with options, you need a platform that's designed for options trading in mind, with excellent charting options, tools like options builders or probability calculators, and fast execution. For instance, Tastytrade is often called a broker "built by options traders, for options traders" because of its top-notch options functionalities. The fact that Tastytrade was established by Tom Sosnoff and Scott Sheridan, two of the pioneers of online options trading, means the platform has been established with options traders' pain points in mind.

On the other hand, if you are a buy-and-hold investor, platforms like Fidelity can serve you best. The broker is known for its extensive stock screeners, detailed analyst reports, and research tools.

Lastly, we think it's okay to have multiple brokerage accounts for your different investing needs. Go for an option-focused broker for CSPs and a long-term focused broker for your buy-and-hold investments.

4. Trading platform features

As an options trader, you need tools like strategy builders, probability calculators, and risk analysis graphs. Plus, you need fast and easy access to option chains with Greeks, fast order entry, and real-time volatility data. Does your broker have all the tools you need? Do you need to pay for the advanced features? If yes, how much is it in comparison with similar brokers?

In our experience, when it comes to trading features in options, two brokers clearly stand out: Interactive Brokers and Tastytrade. Interactive Brokers has professional-grade tools ideal for high-volume options traders. Tastytrade, on the other hand, has an intuitive interface perfect for you when you are starting out. However, if you want to stick to your existing broker, you can use platforms like TradingView for charting, technical analysis, and options strategies.

5. Customer support

If in the name of customer support, all your broker offers is a chatbot that keeps replying in circles, it's probably not a broker that takes customer support seriously. There are times, like when a deposit doesn't get processed in time to place a trade, that you may want to talk to someone with a beating heart. Some brokers provide only email support or ask you to leave your contact details so that they can call you back. In both cases, you may find it hard to resolve issues in real time.

The best brokers are likely to offer multiple options to reach out, including a toll-free number so that you can call and talk to a human being. TastyTrade are particularly well rated for this, as all their phone support is US based. A good way to know about how efficient a particular broker's customer support is by reading reviews on independent platforms like TrustPilot. Yes, there can be some extreme opinions by totally disgruntled customers, but when you read a high number of reviews, you're likely to get a decent idea of the broker.

6. Learning curve, educational resources, and community

If you're just starting out, it makes more sense for you to avoid brokers with a steep learning curve. You can opt for a broker that has a more user-friendly interface, an intuitive design, and a simple trade execution method. Also, if your broker provides learning materials (for example, beginner-friendly tutorials) or has a robust online community, that's a huge advantage. Being active on online forums can help you avoid many beginner's mistakes and learn from your peers.

In addition to the above six factors, look for the regulatory status of your broker. In the US, legitimate brokers are typically regulated by the Securities and Exchange Commission (SEC). Also, they are members of the Financial Industry Regulatory Authority (FINRA). If you are opting for a relatively unknown broker (not recommended, though), check for these regulatory details. And lastly, avoid offshore brokers to avoid any type of fraud.

Now, if you are thinking which are our preferred brokers, we have two: **Tastytrade and Interactive Brokers.** They both are cost-efficient and best suited for options trading. Note that our recommendation is based on our own trading experience and online reviews. We are in no way related to these brokers or get any commission for recommending them.

A few words about setting up your brokerage account

Thanks to competition, it's now easier than ever to open and set up a brokerage account. Most brokers will let you open an account online in under 15 minutes. You'll typically need to provide some basic info related to your identity, address, Social Security number (for U.S. residents), and employment details. Moreover, a broker is likely to ask you a few questions about your trading experience and investing goals to determine if certain types of trades are suitable for you.

Note that most brokers assign options trading permissions in levels, typically from Level 1 to Level 5. Each higher level gives you access to more advanced and risky strategies. Options strategies like covered calls generally come under Level 1. For CSPs, you may need a Level 2 account (this applies to US, UK and Australian traders, for other countries like Canada, you may need a higher level of approval)

To get Level 2 approval, you may need to fill out a form stating your options trading experience, financial situation, and trading objectives.

Once you have opened your account, the next step is to link your bank account for depositing funds. Depending on the broker, it can take a few minutes to 1 or 2 business days to fund your account for the first time. Once you fund your account, you are all set to trade your first CSP.

The next step is to select the right stock.

Key takeaways

◇ It's important to have an option-focused broker for CSPs. They have their platforms optimized for options trading. These brokers also offer tools, fast platforms, and lower costs for frequent traders.

◇ Look for brokers that care about good execution. This can save you a lot of time.

◇ Higher trading fees and commissions can significantly lower your profits. So, look for low-cost options brokers.

◇ Choose a broker that has an easy-to-use and intuitive platform. Moreover, your broker must have great customer support. Read reviews on platforms like Trustpilot to know how customer-friendly your broker is.

Chapter 7

THE $25,000 QUESTION... WHICH STOCKS SHOULD YOU ACTUALLY PICK?

Know what you own, and know why you own it.
- Peter Lynch.

Let me tell you about Rhea's lightbulb moment.

Rhea had been running CSPs for about three months when she emailed me, frustrated. "Oliver," she said, "I'm doing everything right. I'm collecting premiums, managing my positions, following all the rules. But I'm barely breaking even. What am I missing?"

I asked her to send me through her recent trades. Within five minutes, I knew exactly what was wrong.

Rhea had been picking stocks like a kid in a candy store. A little bit of this Electric Vehicle manufacturer because the premium looked juicy. Some of that beaten-down retailer because "it can't go any lower." A dash of that quantum computing stock because she saw a YouTube video touting it as the next big thing.

She was treating stock selection like throwing darts at a board.

"Rhea," I said, "you're optimizing for the wrong thing. You're chasing premiums instead of choosing businesses you'd actually want to own."

Six months later, Rhea emailed me back. She'd done a 180. She'd completely overhauled her approach to stock selection, and her results had transformed. Instead of barely breaking even, she was generating consistent 25%+ annual returns.

The difference? She'd learned to answer the $25,000 question.

The Short Answer vs. The Complete Answer

If you ask me, "How do I select the right stock for CSPs?" I could give you the short answer: "Just pick stocks you don't mind holding."

That's not wrong. It's actually a decent starting point.

But it's incomplete. And incomplete answers lead to incomplete results... like Sarah's original experience.

The complete answer requires understanding something crucial: your CSP profits come from two sources:

1. Premium income when options expire worthless
2. Capital appreciation when you get assigned quality stocks at good prices

The magic happens when you combine both. You want stocks that generate decent premiums AND have the potential to grow your wealth over time.

That's where most people get it wrong. They optimize for one or the other, not both.

The Foundation: Strong Fundamentals (Or Why Boring Beats Exciting)

Here's a truth that might disappoint you, the best CSP candidates are usually boring.

I'm talking about companies like Johnson & Johnson, Procter & Gamble, Coca-Cola. Companies that make products you use every day but never think about. Companies that don't make headlines or go viral on social media.

Why boring? Because boring companies with strong fundamentals tend to:

◇ Grow steadily over time (J&J and P&G have delivered 10%+ annualized returns over the past decade)

◇ Survive market crashes better than flashy growth stocks

◇ Generate consistent cash flows that support their stock prices

◇ Give you peace of mind when you get assigned

When legendary investors like Warren Buffett and Peter Lynch say "buy the business, not the stock," this is what they mean. You want to own pieces of real businesses that make real money, not lottery tickets.

The Fundamental Checklist: What to Look For

When I'm evaluating a potential CSP candidate, I look for several key factors…

1. Consistent Earnings Growth - I want companies that grow their profits year after year. Not necessarily explosive growth (that often comes with explosive volatility), but steady, predictable increases.

Look at the "boring" businesses: Johnson & Johnson, Procter & Gamble, Coca-Cola, PepsiCo, Colgate-Palmolive. They rarely make headlines, but they consistently post higher earnings and reward shareholders.

2. High Return on Equity (ROE) - ROE tells you how efficiently a company uses shareholder money to generate profits. Amazon's ROE of 25.28% means they generate $25.28 in profit for every $100 of shareholder equity.

My rule of thumb...

ROE above 15% = good

ROE above 30% = very strong

ROE below 10% = proceed with caution

3. Manageable Debt Levels - I look at the debt-to-equity (D/E) ratio to see how much debt a company carries relative to its equity.

Different industries have different norms (telecom companies naturally carry more debt), but generally:

D/E below 1.0 = safe

D/E above 2.0 = risky territory

4. Positive Free Cash Flow - Free cash flow (FCF) shows how much cash a company generates after paying all expenses. This is the money available for dividends, debt repayment, or reinvestment.

Apple's $98 billion in free cash flow? That's a company with options. A company bleeding cash? That's a company with problems.

5. The Dividend Consideration - Here's where it gets interesting. Dividend income can boost your total returns, but there's a catch.

High-growth companies often reinvest profits instead of paying dividends. Amazon has never paid a dividend. Apple yields only 0.49%. Meanwhile, Coca-Cola yields 2.85% and Verizon yields 6.20%.

Neither approach is wrong. If you want dividend income (once you get assigned the stock) on top of your CSP premiums, look for sustainable yields in the 1-3% range. If you're focused purely on growth and premium income, dividend yield becomes irrelevant.

The Economic Moat: Your Secret Weapon

Beyond the numbers, I look for something harder to quantify but incredibly valuable: economic moats.

An economic moat is whatever gives a company a sustainable competitive advantage. It might be:

◇ Brand power (Coca-Cola, Apple)

◇ Network effects (Facebook, Visa)

◇ Cost advantages (Walmart, Costco)

◇ Regulatory barriers (utilities, railroads)

◇ Switching costs (Microsoft, Oracle)

Companies with strong moats tend to maintain their competitive positions over time, which translates to more predictable stock performance... exactly what we want for CSPs.

Note: If you're interested in learning more about the concept of moats, and the kinds of stocks that have them, check out one of our other books **Fantastic Moats and Where to Find Them**

Putting It All Together

Now, let's look at some potential CSP candidates (large-cap, well-established companies) with the fundamental ratios we discussed above:

Please note: Stock price and market cap data are accurate as of Apil 17th, 2025

Compa-ny	Stock Price (USD)	Market Cap (USD B)	P/E Ra-tio	Free Cash Flow Yield	Divi-dend Yield	ROE
Johnson & John-son (JNJ)	$156.12	$392.08	17.23	5.62%	2.9%	29.95%
Procter & Gam-ble (PG)	$160.52	$397.92	23.78	4.06%	2.4%	32.0%
Coca-Co-la (KO)	$71.65	$307.22	28.9	-0.31%	2.9%	41.9%
PepsiCo (PEP)	$133.75	$211.00	25.5	4.11%	2.8%	48.7%
Mic-rosoft (MSFT)	$435.28	$2,790.64	28.88	1.94%	0.8%	39%
Apple (AAPL)	$205.35	$3,280.73	33.72	3.35%	0.49%	29.95%
Verizon (VZ)	$43.54	$183.56	10.41	11.81%	6.7%	32%
Amazon (AMZN)	$186.35	$1,980	31.09	0.92%	0%	30.5%

Table 4: Potential large-cap CSP candidates

If all these ratios look intimidating, it's okay.

You don't need to dig through balance sheets and income statements to find out your perfect picks for CSPs. Stock screening platforms like Finviz and stockanalysis.com can help you find stocks based on your criteria. Go to 'finviz.com', select "Screener" and then click on the tab "Fundamental" to sort stocks based on any fundamental criteria you want.

*(**Disclaimer***: *Freeman Publications is in no way connected to Finviz or stockanalysis.com)*

Once you have a solid list of fundamentally strong companies, technical analysis becomes your timing tool. It helps you answer the crucial question: "Is now a good time to sell puts on this stock?"

Technical Analysis: The When to Your What

If fundamental analysis tells you **what** stocks to pick, technical analysis tells you **when** to sell CSPs on them.

This timing component is what separates consistently profitable CSP traders from those who struggle. You can pick the best companies in the world, but if your timing is off, your results will suffer.

Price Trend: Your First Filter

The first thing I examine is simple: Which direction is the stock moving?

Is it trending up? Moving sideways in a range? Or heading down?

For CSPs, you want stocks that are either:

◇ Moving sideways in a trading range

◇ Trending gently upward

Why Sideways Movement is Perfect

When a stock trades sideways, it creates ideal conditions for CSP traders:

◇ Your puts are more likely to expire out of the money (you keep the premium)

◇ You can sell puts closer to the current price, which means higher premiums

◇ The stock isn't going anywhere fast, so time decay works in your favor

When a stock is moving sideways, you can safely sell ATM or slight OTM puts without excessive risk.

Why Gentle Uptrends Work Too

Upward-trending stocks give you the best of both worlds

◇ Good chance your puts expire worthless (you keep premiums)

◇ If you do get assigned, you're buying a stock that's appreciating

The key word here is "gentle." You want steady, sustainable uptrends, not parabolic moves that are due for a crash.

What to Avoid: Downtrending Stocks

This should be obvious, but it's worth emphasizing: avoid stocks in clear downtrends.

When you sell puts on falling stocks, you're fighting gravity. Your puts are more likely to finish in the money, meaning you'll get assigned shares of a declining company.

That's not just financially painful... it's psychologically brutal. Nobody wants to watch their newly assigned shares lose value day after day.

The Volatility Sweet Spot

Next, I examine volatility, specifically implied volatility (IV).

IV tells you how much the market expects a stock to move in the near future. It's expressed as a percentage:

◇ Below 20% = low volatility

◇ 20-55% = moderate volatility

◇ Above 60% = high volatility

Here's the dilemma every options seller faces: higher IV means higher premiums. It's tempting to chase those attractive premiums on high-volatility stocks.

But high volatility usually means high risk. Those stocks with 80% IV and mouth-watering premiums? They're volatile for a reason. Maybe they're meme stocks. Maybe they have earnings coming up. Maybe they're in a declining industry.

For CSPs, I target the sweet spot: 25-55% IV. This range provides decent premiums without the extreme volatility that can destroy your account.

It's the middle path... not too boring, not too exciting.

RSI: The Momentum Check

The Relative Strength Index (RSI) is a momentum indicator that ranges from 0 to 100. It tells you whether a stock is overbought or oversold:

◇ RSI above 70 = overbought (stock may be due for a pullback)

◇ RSI below 30 = oversold (stock may be due for a bounce)

◇ RSI between 30-70 = neutral territory

For CSPs, I avoid both extremes. Overbought stocks can suddenly reverse and crash through your strike price. Oversold stocks might be oversold for good reason.

I stick to the RSI sweet spot of 30-70. This helps me avoid stocks that are due for violent price swings in either direction.

The Golden Rule: Avoid Surprises

Everything we've covered serves one purpose: avoiding sudden, unpredictable price swings.

That's the enemy of successful CSP trading. You want boring, predictable stocks that move in gentle, sustainable patterns. You want to sleep peacefully knowing your positions aren't going to gap against you overnight.

Your Technical Screening Tool

For technical screening, TradingView.com is what I personally use. It offers filters for RSI, moving averages, volatility, and other key indicators we'll cover in the next chapter.

The power of combining fundamental and technical analysis is that you end up with a refined list of high-quality candidates at optimal entry points.

The Complete Picture So Far

We've established that the best CSP candidates are:

◇ Large-cap companies (market cap > $10 billion)

◇ Fundamentally strong and "boring"

◇ Trading sideways or in gentle uptrends

◇ Moderate volatility (IV 25-55%)

◇ Neutral momentum (RSI 30-70)

Remember one thing we always want to avoid in options trading in general and CSPs in particular: the risk of sudden, unpredictable price swings.

In the next chapter, we'll explore additional technical indicators like moving averages and chart patterns that can further refine your timing and selection process.

Because picking great stocks is only half the battle. Timing your entries is what separates profitable CSP traders from those who struggle to generate consistent returns.

And if you'd like to see some live case studies on the kinds of stocks I like for Cash Secured Puts - I've uploaded a bunch of them on my YouTube channel

<u>freemanpublications.com/youtube</u>

Key takeaways

◇ For CSPs, pick fundamentally strong stocks with great earnings, low debt, and large capitalization. These are the stocks you would like to own in the long run.

◇ The best stocks for CSPs are large-cap stocks with low volatility and stable returns.

◇ Look for technical factors like price trend, RSI, and IV to time your trades and maximize premium income without taking excessive risks.

Chapter 8

TECHNICAL ANALYSIS FOR CSPS (EASIER THAN YOU THINK)

"You don't make money by trading, you make it by sitting. It takes patience to wait for the trade to develop and for the opportunity to present itself. Let the market come to you, instead of chasing the market. Chart patterns are very accurate. They have proven their accuracy and predictability time and time again, but you have to wait for them to develop."
- Fred McAllen.

It's 1952, and a ballroom dancer named Nicolas Darvas has just finished a performance in Toronto. As payment for his show, he receives shares in a small mining company instead of cash.

Most people would have been annoyed. Darvas was intrigued.

Within weeks, those shares doubled in value. Darvas was hooked, but not in the way you might expect. He didn't rush out to buy more mining stocks or start reading annual reports. Instead, he did something different.

"I decided to treat the stock market like a scientific experiment," he later wrote.

For the next several years, while touring the world as a dancer, Darvas studied price patterns, volume, and big price moves. He watched the market dance while trying to find patterns in its movements.

The result? He turned less than $25,000 into $2 million in under two years, documenting his journey in the investment classic *"How I Made $2,000,000 in the Stock Market."*

What Darvas was doing was technical analysis... looking at price movements to predict the market's next moves. And he did it all without knowing what those companies actually did or who ran them.

Figure 5: Nicolas Darvas (left) (Source: trendfollowing.com)

The Great Technical Analysis Debate

Technical analysis, or "charting" as it's informally called, is one of the most polarizing topics in investing.

Academics call it "voodoo finance." Long-term investors often dismiss it entirely. But millions of traders, especially options traders, swear by it.

Then there's a third group... people who think technical analysis is too complicated to understand or apply.

If you're in that third camp, this chapter is for you. We're going to break down the key technical concepts that actually matter for CSP trading, and we'll do it in a way that's simple and practical.

Support and resistance 101

Support and Resistance: The Market's Floor and Ceiling

When selling CSPs, you want to know how far a stock might move in the short term. Support and resistance levels help you figure out a stock's likely trading range.

Think of support as the floor and resistance as the ceiling.

Let's look at a real example: In late 2024 and early 2025, Nvidia was trading between roughly $122 and $144. The stock bounced up from $122 multiple times (support) while failing to break above $144 (resistance).

Figure 6: *NVIDIA Support and Resistance (Source: TradingView)*

81

Why Do These Levels Exist?

It's basic Economics 101: supply and demand.

Support is the demand zone. When a stock hits these levels, buyers step in because they see value. This buying pressure pushes the price back up.

Resistance is the supply zone. When a stock reaches these levels, sellers take profits or cut losses, creating selling pressure that pushes the price back down.

Once a stock bounces off a certain level, traders expect similar behavior next time. They buy near support and sell near resistance. As more people do this, these levels become self-fulfilling prophecies.

How to Use Support and Resistance for CSPs

Here's the practical application: support and resistance help you pick better strike prices.

If Nvidia has support at $122 and resistance at $144, selling a $122 put is a safer bet because there's lower probability of the option finishing in the money.

Key Points to Remember:

⋄ Support and resistance are zones, not exact prices

⋄ There can be multiple levels of each

⋄ These levels eventually break (nothing lasts forever)

⋄ When resistance breaks, it often becomes new support (and vice versa)

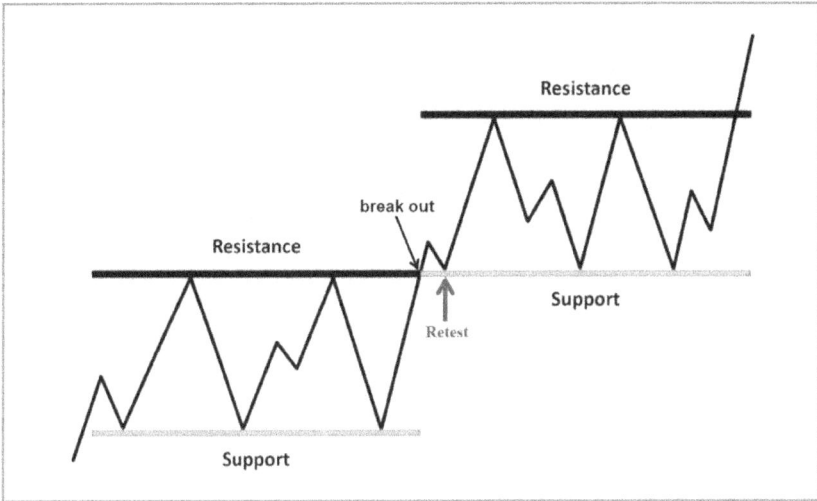

Figure 7: *Resistance turning into support (Source: Medium)*

So, why are supports and resistances important in selling CSPs?

Trend Identification: Your Friend Until the End

As trading legend Ed Seykota said: "The trend is your friend until the end when it bends."

Trends come in three flavors:

◇ **Uptrend:** Higher highs and higher lows

◇ **Downtrend:** Lower highs and lower lows

◇ **Sideways:** Moving within a defined range

For CSPs, you want stocks that are either trending up or moving sideways. Avoid downtrending stocks like the plague.

Why Trends Matter

When a stock is in an uptrend, there's lower probability your put will finish in the money.

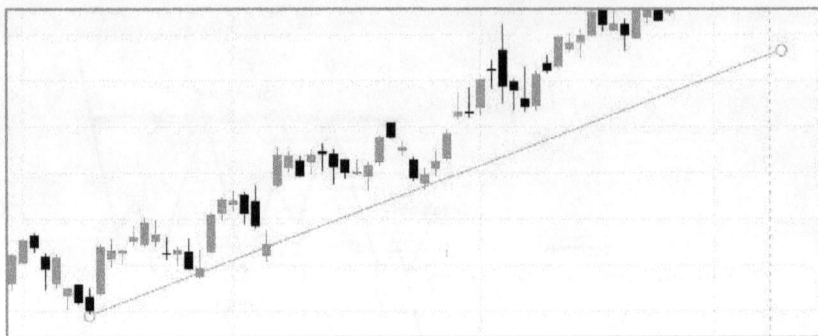

Figure 8: *Uptrend (Source: TradingView)*

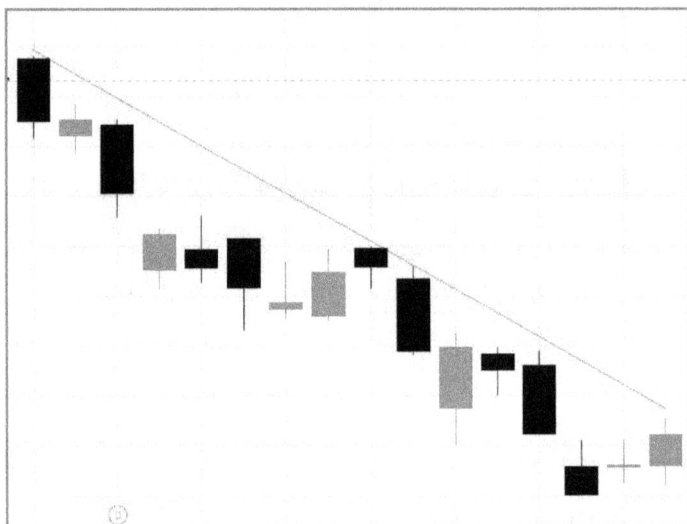

Figure 9: *Downtrend (Source: Tradingview)*

For sideways-moving stocks, you can sell puts near support levels with confidence.

Downtrending stocks are dangerous because they can break through multiple support levels, leaving you with big unrealized losses on assigned shares.

Volume Confirms Everything

Always study trends in combination with volume. Higher volume makes trends stronger and more reliable.

When a stock rises on heavy volume, the uptrend is robust. When it falls on heavy volume, the correction is likely to continue.

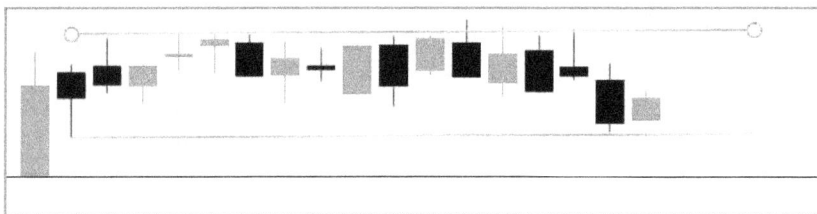

Figure 10: Sideways trend (Source: Tradingview)

Stocks tend to stay in a sideways phase after a major uptrend or downtrend. In that sense, a range-bound market shows a consolidation phase before the beginning of a new up or downtrend.

Moving Averages: Smoothing Out the Noise

Moving averages might sound technical, but they're actually one of the simplest tools in technical analysis. They can help you...

◇ Confirm trends

◇ Filter out daily market noise

◇ Identify potential breakouts or breakdowns

◇ Find support levels

There are 2 types of moving averages that you should know.

Simple Moving Average (SMA): Average closing price over X days

Exponential Moving Average (EMA): Gives more weight to recent prices (reacts faster)

For CSPs, focus on shorter-term EMAs like the 20-day or 50-day.

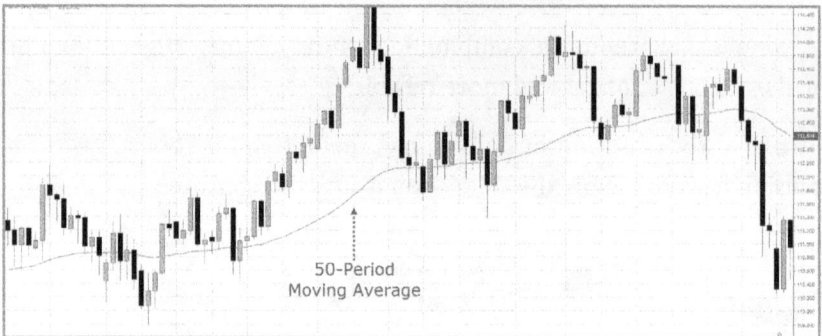

Figure 11: *50-day moving average (Source: tradingwithrayner.com)*

How Moving Averages Help Your CSP Trading:

1. Trend Confirmation: Stock consistently above its 50-day EMA = uptrend

2. Breakout Identification: Stock breaking above EMA with volume = potential breakout

3. Support Levels: Stock bouncing off EMA = EMA acting as support

4. Major Trend Changes: Golden crossover (short-term MA crosses above long-term) = bullish signal

The Golden Setup

An ideal CSP setup: a stock bouncing off its 20-day EMA while trading well above its 200-day EMA. This suggests short-term bullishness within a long-term uptrend.

RSI: The Momentum Gauge

The Relative Strength Index (RSI) tells you whether buyers or sellers are in control. It ranges from 0 to 100:

⋄ RSI below 30 = oversold (sellers dominating)

⋄ RSI above 70 = overbought (buyers euphoric)

⋄ RSI 30-70 = sweet spot for CSPs

The CSP Sweet Spot

Look for fundamentally strong stocks with RSI between 30-50. This suggests selling pressure has eased but the stock isn't overbought yet.

Avoid stocks with RSI above 70. Buyer enthusiasm may be peaking, setting up potential reversals.

Putting It All Together

Technical analysis isn't about predicting the future with certainty. It's about stacking probabilities in your favor.

As Nicolas Darvas learned, you have to "accept everything for what it was, not what I wanted it to be."

The market has no obligation to respect support levels or complete chart patterns. But by combining these tools, you can make more informed decisions about when and where to sell your CSPs.

The Patient Approach

Remember Darvas's wisdom: "I just stayed on the sidelines and waited for better times to come."

Don't force trades. Let clear patterns emerge. Wait for confirmations. The best CSP opportunities come to those who wait for the right setup.

In the next chapter, we'll explore volatility and why chasing those tempting high premiums isn't always the smart play.

Key takeaways

◇ Support and resistance help you identify the short-term trading range of a stock. Sell CSPs near strong support zones.

◇ Identify the underlying trend and trade in the direction of the trend. Never fight the trend. Stocks in uptrends or a stage of sideways consolidation make great CSP candidates.

◇ Confirm the trend using moving averages. Keep an eye on moving average crossovers.

◇ RSI shows whether a stock is overbought, oversold, or somewhere in between. An RSI between 30-50 can be a sweet spot, provided that you consider other factors.

Chapter 9

THE VIX... WALL STREET'S FEAR GAUGE

"It is said that the present is pregnant with the future."
- Voltaire

April 2, 2025. The White House Rose Garden.

President Trump steps up to the podium for what he's calling "Liberation Day." Within minutes, he announces aggressive tariffs ranging from 10-49% on imports from countries around the world.

The market's reaction was swift and brutal.

Over the next four trading days, the S&P 500 plummeted from 5,670 to 4,982... a gut-wrenching 12% drop that wiped out trillions in market value.

But while most investors watched their portfolios bleed red, another index was having the time of its life. This mysterious index spiked over 140%, rocketing from 21.51 to 52.33.

That index? The VIX.

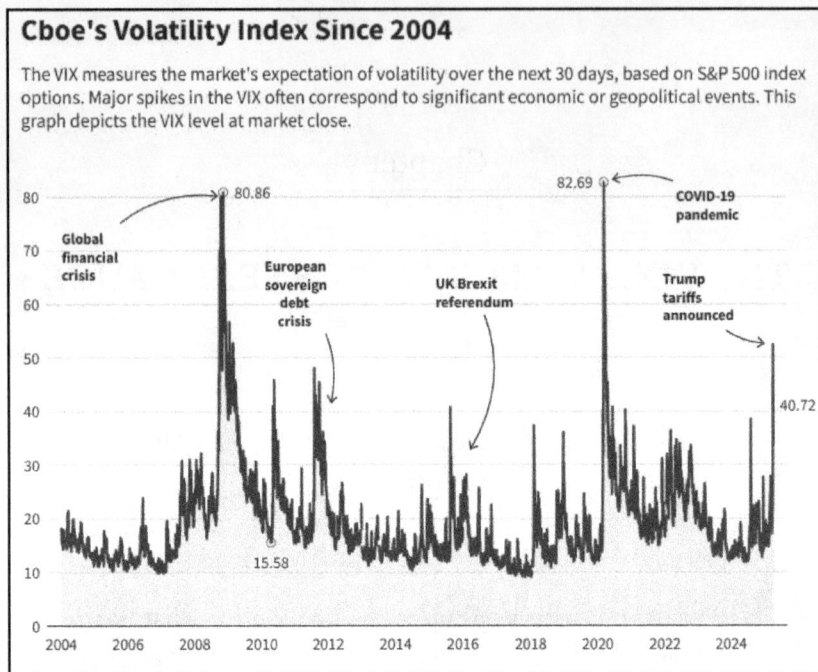

Figure 12: VIX index since 2004 (Source: Investopedia)

Wall Street calls it the "Fear Gauge," and for good reason. The VIX feeds on investor anxiety like a vampire feeds on blood. The more terrified investors become, the higher it climbs.

The VIX's Greatest Hits

The VIX has a long history of showing up at the worst possible moments:

March 2020: When COVID-19 brought the world economy to its knees, the VIX spiked to a spine-chilling 82.69

October 2008: During the subprime mortgage crisis, it hit an intraday high of 89.53

Every market crash since 1993: The VIX has been there, like the Grim Reaper delivering news of financial death and destruction

The values of the VIX and how to interpret them

Theoretically, the value of the VIX can get as low as near-zero (it can't really touch zero because there is always some amount of uncertainty in the market). There is no theoretical upper limit of the VIX, as there is no limit to chaos in the market. But if we go by history, the lowest intraday value the VIX ever experienced is 8.56 on November 24, 2017. On the higher side, as we mentioned earlier in the chapter, the VIX reached its all-time high mark of 89.53% in 2008. Putting the extremes aside, the average value of the VIX has remained nearly 19 in the 10-year period between 2015 and 2025.

For example, on May 15, 2025 the VIX sat at 19.14.

Some of my might be asking, "What does 19.14 actually represent?"

When the value of VIX is 19.14, it means that the market is expecting the S&P 500 index to go up or down by an *annualized* rate of 19.14% over the next 30 days. This also means there is a 68% probability (one standard deviation) that:

◇ The S&P 500 will move up or down by about 5.5% over the next month.

◇ And, by 2.65% over the next week.

The Math:

$$19.14\% \times \sqrt{(30/365)} \approx 5.5\%.$$

$$19.14\% \times \sqrt{(7/365)} \approx 2.6\%$$

Let's see how an increase in the VIX changes these expectations of future volatility. Let's say the VIX more than doubles from 19.14% to 40%. The market now expects an annualized volatility of 40% for the S&P 500 over the next 30 days. This also means there is now a 68% probability that the market can go up or down by 11.5% in the next month and by 5.4% in the next week.

Why Should CSP Traders Care About the VIX?

Here's the thing: as an options trader, you can't afford to ignore the VIX. It doesn't just affect the broader market... it directly impacts the volatility and option premiums of individual stocks.

Understanding the VIX is like having a weather forecast for the options market. And just like you wouldn't plan a picnic during a hurricane warning, you shouldn't sell CSPs when the VIX is screaming danger.

What Exactly Is the VIX?

Let's demystify this beast.

The VIX stands for the CBOE Volatility Index (CBOE being the Chicago Board Options Exchange, the largest options exchange in the US). Introduced in 1993 and revamped in 2003, the VIX measures one thing: how much volatility the market expects over the next 30 days.

Think of it this way: The CBOE takes a basket of S&P 500 options, analyzes their prices, and calculates what investors expect the market to do. When people are buying expensive options as insurance against big moves, the VIX rises. When everyone's calm and options are cheap, the VIX falls.

The VIX Translation Guide

Here's how to read the VIX like a pro:

VIX below 20: Market is calm, investors are complacent

VIX 20-30: Normal volatility, typical market conditions

VIX 30-40: Elevated fear, investors getting nervous

VIX above 40: Panic mode, investors expecting major moves

Why the VIX Matters for Your CSP Strategy

When the VIX spikes, several things happen that directly affect your CSP trades:

1. Option Premiums Explode: High VIX means high implied volatility across the board. Those juicy premiums you see during market turmoil? That's the VIX at work.

2. Assignment Risk Increases: Volatile markets mean stocks can gap down overnight, blowing through your strike prices before you can react.

3. Correlation Goes to 1: During VIX spikes, individual stock movements become highly correlated. Your carefully diversified CSP portfolio suddenly moves in lockstep.

The Temptation Trap

Here's where many CSP traders get into trouble: they see those fat premiums during high VIX periods and think, "This is my chance to make a killing!"

It's like seeing a $100 bill lying in the middle of a busy highway. Sure, it's tempting, but the risk of getting run over isn't worth it.

The Smart VIX Strategy for CSP Traders

When VIX is Low (Below 20):

◇ Premium hunting becomes harder

◇ Markets are generally stable

◇ Good time for steady, consistent CSP income

◇ Focus on quality stocks with reasonable premiums

When VIX is Moderate (20-30):

◇ Sweet spot for CSP trading

◇ Decent premiums without excessive risk

◇ Normal market conditions

◇ Your bread-and-butter trading environment

When VIX is Elevated (30-40):

◇ Proceed with extreme caution

◇ Premiums look attractive but risk is high

◇ Consider reducing position sizes

◇ Focus only on your highest-conviction plays

When VIX is in Panic Mode (Above 40):

◇ Step away from the keyboard

◇ Resist the temptation of huge premiums

◇ Wait for the storm to pass

◇ Use cash to buy quality stocks directly if you must do something

The 20/20 rule

Smart CSP traders follow what's called the "20-20 rule" when markets get choppy:

When the VIX climbs above 20, stick to put options with a delta of 20 or lower.

This simple rule does two things:

Lowers your assignment risk to roughly 20% or less

Still captures decent premiums because volatility is elevated

You're essentially trading some premium income for better odds of keeping that premium.

The Risk-Reward Balance

At the end of the day, successful CSP trading is all about balancing risk and reward. High VIX periods offer tempting premiums, but they come with elevated risk. The 20-20 rule helps you stay in the game without betting the farm.

Remember: it's better to make consistent smaller profits than to swing for the fences and strike out when volatility spikes.

The VIX Reality Check

Remember: the VIX isn't predicting what will happen... it's measuring what people think might happen. Sometimes the market overreacts. Sometimes it underreacts.

But here's what history tells us: VIX spikes don't last forever. They're like thunderstorms... intense while they're happening, but they eventually pass.

Your VIX Action Plan

◇ Monitor the VIX daily (it's free on any financial website)

◇ Adjust your CSP strategy based on VIX levels

◇ Resist FOMO when premiums spike during high VIX periods

◇ Be patient and wait for favorable conditions to return

The Bottom Line

The VIX is like that friend who only calls when there's drama. Most of the time, you can ignore it. But when it starts screaming, you better pay attention.

As a CSP trader, your goal isn't to predict when the VIX will spike or crash. Your goal is to recognize when market conditions favor your strategy and when they don't.

The VIX gives you that insight. Use it wisely, and it can save you from costly mistakes. Ignore it, and you might find yourself holding a portfolio full of underwater positions wondering what went wrong.

In the next chapter, we'll dive into the Greeks... those mysterious factors that determine option prices and can make or break your CSP trades.

Key takeaways

◇ The VIX, the "fear gauge" of the market, tells you the expected volatility of the S&P 500.

◇ A higher level of the VIX is associated with higher expected volatility.

◇ Higher VIX often leads to higher options prices. However, a higher VIX level also means there is now a greater chance of assignment.

◇ A VIX range of 15-25 balances risks and rewards well. However, adjust your strike price if you want to trade under higher volatility.

◇ Follow the 20-20 rule to pick options when the VIX is greater than 2o. Under this rule, you need to sell puts with a delta of 20 to lower the probability of assignments.

Chapter 10

THE GREEKS... YOUR OPTIONS GPS SYSTEM

"If you want to be an options trader, you have to understand that options are not just bets — they are contracts whose value depends on many moving parts"
- **Myron Scholes.**

It's 1971, and a half-blind professor at MIT is wrestling with a problem that's been stumping Wall Street for decades.

Myron Scholes couldn't see well, but as he later said, his impaired vision made him exceptional at listening and thinking. And the problem he was thinking about? A simple yet profound question:

"What are options truly worth?"

At the time, options traders were basically making educated guesses. Some guy on the trading floor would look at an option and say, "Eh, feels like it's worth about three bucks." Another trader might think it was worth five. Nobody really knew.

Scholes teamed up with his colleague Fischer Black, and for the next year and a half, they worked on cracking this code. In 1973, they published the Black-Scholes formula... a mathematical breakthrough that would eventually earn Scholes a Nobel Prize and revolutionize finance forever.

The Timing Was Perfect

Here's the beautiful coincidence: the exact same year Scholes and Black published their formula, the Chicago Board Options Exchange launched stock options trading in the US. Suddenly, professional traders armed with mathematical precision were competing against floor traders relying on gut instinct.

Guess who won?

The traders using the Black-Scholes formula gradually outcompeted the old-school intuition-based traders. It was like bringing calculators to an abacus competition.

Beyond Just Pricing

The Black-Scholes formula uses variables like stock price, strike price, time to expiration, volatility, and interest rates to calculate what an option should be worth. But here's where it gets really interesting...

Using some sophisticated math (don't worry, we're not going there), we can figure out how an option's value changes when any of these factors move. These sensitivities are expressed through what we call the "Greeks."

Why Should You Care About the Greeks?

Think of the Greeks as your options GPS system. Just like GPS tells you not just where you are, but which direction you're heading and how fast, the Greeks tell you not just what your option is worth, but how that value will change under different conditions.

As a CSP trader, you need to understand questions like:

"What happens to my put's value if the stock drops $5?"

"How much will I lose if volatility suddenly spikes?"

"How much money am I making each day just from time passing?"

The Greeks answer all these questions and more.

The Essential Greeks for CSP Traders

There are five main Greeks, but we'll focus on the four that actually matter for CSP trading:

Delta (Δ): How much your option's value changes when the stock price moves

Gamma (Γ): How much your delta changes when the stock price moves

Theta (Θ): How much your option loses value each day due to time decay

Vega: How much your option's value changes when volatility moves

(There's also Rho, which measures sensitivity to interest rate changes, but it's largely irrelevant for our purposes.)

What's beautiful about modern trading, is that you don't need to calculate any of this stuff manually. Your trading platform does all the heavy lifting. The Black-Scholes formula and all its derivatives are built right into every major options platform.

You just need to understand what the numbers mean and how to use them to make better trading decisions.

Delta (Δ): Your Assignment Probability Meter

Delta is the most important Greek you'll ever encounter as a CSP trader. Think of it as your assignment probability meter.

Here's how it works: Delta tells you how much your option's price changes when the stock moves $1.

Let's say Bank of America is trading at $45, and you're looking at the $40 strike options:

◇ The $40 call has a delta of 0.88

◇ The $40 put has a delta of -0.09

If BAC moves up $1 to $46:

◇ The call option gains $0.88 in value

◇ The put option loses $0.09 in value

If BAC drops $1 to $39:

◇ The call option loses $0.88 in value

◇ The put option gains $0.09 in value

Delta's Secret Power: Assignment Probability

Here's where Delta becomes incredibly useful for CSP traders: it roughly tells you the probability of your option finishing in the money.

A 20 delta put? About 20% chance of assignment. A 50 delta put? About 50% chance of assignment.

This isn't mathematically exact, but it's close enough to be your go-to rule of thumb.

Key Delta Facts:

Calls: Delta ranges from 0 to 1

Puts: Delta ranges from 0 to -1

At-the-money options: Delta around 0.5

Deep in-the-money: Delta approaches 1 (or -1 for puts)

Far out-of-the-money: Delta approaches 0

For CSPs, you typically want to sell puts with 20-30 delta. This gives you decent premium income while keeping assignment risk manageable.

Delta Slang

If delta ranges between 0 and 1 for call options, why do you sometimes hear people (including myself) refer to "20 delta" or "50 delta"

Simply because it's easier to say and less open to interpretation errors than saying "zero point two delta"

So 0.2 delta will often be referred to as 20 delta in conversation.

0.5 delta will be 50 delta

0.9 delta will be 90 delta

I hope that helps!

Gamma (Γ): Delta's Rate of Change

Here's the thing about Delta: it's not static. As the stock price moves, Delta changes too. Gamma tells you how fast.

If you have a put with -0.50 delta and 0.05 gamma, and the stock rises $1, your new delta becomes -0.45.

Why Gamma Matters for CSP Traders:

Highest at-the-money: ATM options have the most gamma

Risk indicator: High gamma means your delta (and option price) can change rapidly

Another reason to go OTM: Out-of-the-money puts have lower gamma, meaning more predictable behavior

Think of gamma as the "acceleration" of your option's price movement. Lower gamma means smoother, more predictable changes.

Theta (Θ): Your Daily Paycheck

Theta is your best friend as an options seller. It tells you how much money you make each day just from time passing.

If your put has a theta of -0.04, you're collecting $4 per day per contract in time decay (assuming nothing else changes).

Theta's Behavior:

Always negative: Both calls and puts lose value over time

Highest for ATM options: At-the-money options decay fastest

Accelerates near expiration: Options lose about 1/3 of their value in the first half of their life, 2/3 in the second half

The Sweet Spot for CSPs is sell options with <u>21-45 days to expiration</u>.

This gives you:

◇ Decent premium income upfront

◇ Accelerating time decay as expiration approaches

◇ Enough time to manage positions if needed

Vega: The Volatility Wild Card

Vega tells you how much your option's value changes when implied volatility moves 1%.

If your put has a vega of 0.01 and volatility increases 1%, your option gains $1 in value.

Why This Matters: When you sell a put and volatility spikes (like during market crashes), your option becomes more expensive. That's bad for you as the seller because it increases your potential loss if you need to buy back the option.

This is another reason to avoid selling puts when the VIX is elevated, but declining.

Rho (ρ): The Forgotten Greek

Rho measures sensitivity to interest rate changes. For CSP traders, it's largely irrelevant. Interest rates don't change daily, and when they do change, the effect on your short-term options is minimal.

Finding the Greeks: No Math Required

The beautiful thing about modern trading? You don't need to calculate any of this. Every decent trading platform shows you the Greeks right in the options chain.

Just look up your stock on your broker's platform or a site like Nasdaq.com, and you'll see all the Greeks calculated for you.

The Bottom Line

There's no one-size-fits-all CSP strategy. The Greeks give you the data points to make informed decisions, but your risk tolerance and trading goals determine how you use that data.

Conservative traders might stick to 20 delta puts far out of the money, accepting lower premiums for lower risk. Aggressive traders might sell 40-50 delta puts closer to the money for higher premiums.

The key is taking calculated risks based on your situation, not flying blind.

What's Next

Now that you understand the fundamentals, the technical analysis, the VIX, and the Greeks, it's time to put it all together.

In the next chapter, we'll walk through executing your first CSP trade step by step, combining everything you've learned into a practical, actionable strategy.

Key takeaways

◇ The option Greeks help you understand how different factors affect option prices.

◇ Delta tells you how much an option's price changes when the stock moves by $1. For CSPs, we prefer low delta puts (20–30) to lower the risk of assignment.

◇ Gamma shows how fast delta changes with stock price movements.

◇ Theta shows time decay and tells you how fast an option loses value each day. For CSPs, we prefer selling puts with 21–45 days to expiry.

Chapter 11

A STEP-BY-STEP GUIDE TO EXECUTING YOUR FIRST CSP

"The secret of getting ahead is getting started"
- Mark Twain.

They say that the first step is always the hardest. The journey gets smoother as you keep going. So, it may feel a bit overwhelming to combine and implement everything we learned so far and execute your first CSP. However, taking a step-by-step approach can help you simplify this process. In this chapter, we are going to revisit the basic steps in executing a CSP trade so that you can start your CSP journey right away.

Let's begin with the first step:

Step 1: Analyzing the market conditions

Remember to always start by looking at the overall market conditions. CSPs work best when the larger market is in a bullish or a consolidating phase. You don't want to defy the overall market trend, as individual stocks (especially the large-cap stocks we want to pick for CSPs) tend to mimic the index.

As of the writing of this chapter in the 3rd week of May 2025, the S&P 500 is showing a bullish trend. The market has delivered a return of over 10% in the last 30 days. The current VIX is 20.28, which means the volatility level is medium. So, the current market suits our criteria and is ripe for CSPs. (**Note:** Avoid CSPs if the larger market is bearish and/ or the VIX is greater than 30. In April 2025, the VIX remained above 30 for quite some time due to tariff announcements. This was a reason we didn't initiate any new trade during the month). We can now move to the next step of selecting the right stock.

Step 2: Select the right stock

Use a stock screener like Finviz to shortlist a basket of stocks. We can then further reduce the basket to a single stock or 2-3 stocks based on your trading approach (a single position vs. a portfolio approach).

A good screener like Finviz will allow you to set both fundamental and technical criteria to shortlist stocks. Here are some of the basic, fundamental, and technical criteria to begin with:

◇ **Fundamental:** We prefer large-cap (market cap > $10 billion) and low to moderate PE stocks, which can offer stable growth without wild price swings. Consider dividend yield, too, if generating dividend income is a part of your long-term investing strategy.

◇ **Technical:** Use technical criteria like the Relative Strength Index (RSI), volatility, moving averages, and performance (rate of return in the last week or month to know the trend). We have discussed these criteria before in the book. Just to revise the basics: Look for stocks in the RSI range of 30 to 70, implied volatility of 30-55, and stocks that are currently trading over the 50-day and 200-day moving averages.

Once you have a set of stocks meeting your fundamental and technical criteria, fine-tune the list based on the current trend (to do this, review the 3-month chart using 1-hour candles), stock price (since your cash requirement depends on the stock price), and if the stock is trading near a major support level. Remember that we want to execute CSPs on a stock showing an uptrend or bullish consolidation.

Based on the above criteria, we found Bank of America (BAC), among several others, a suitable choice. BAC is a large-cap (market cap: 326.21 billion), low PE stock (PE ratio: 12.89). With a current price of $43.31, BAC is trading above both the 50 and 200-day moving averages, which show a strong uptrend. Moreover, the stock is trading near a short-term support zone around $43. On top of all these, recently, a golden crossover happened in the stock when the 50-day moving average crossed over the 200-day moving average.

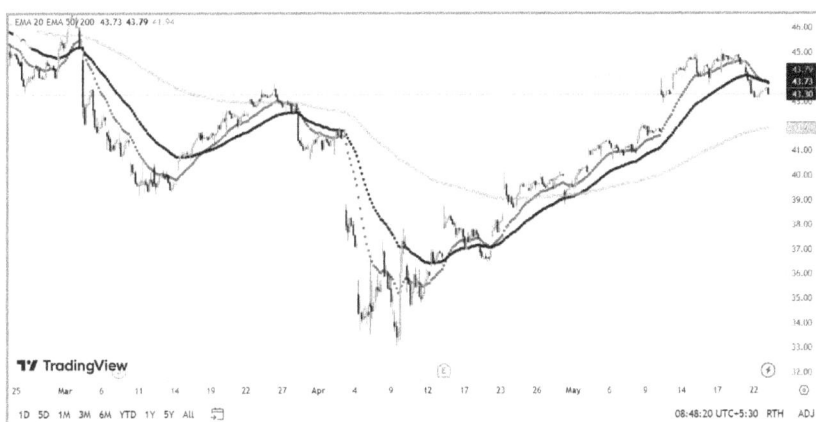

Figure 13: BAC hourly chart (Source: TradingView)

Once you have settled on a stock, the next step is to look at its option chain and select the right strike price and expiration date.

Step 3: Selecting strike prices and expiration dates

While selecting strike prices and expiration dates, our main goal is to maximize the premium income without aggressive risk-taking. For expiration date, a good rule of thumb is to select options having 21 to 45 days to expire. So, based on today's date (May 22, 2025), we are going to pick the June 20, 2025, expiration date. This gives us 29 days until expiration.

Now, for the strike price, delta and IV are some of our main criteria. A good rule of thumb for a low-risk CSP trade is to pick a put option with a delta between 20 to 30 and an IV of 30% to 55%.

Date	Jun 20, 2025 ▾											
Calls							**Puts**					
Delta	**Gamma**	**Rho**	**Theta**	**Vega**	**IV**	**Strike**	**Delta**	**Gamma**	**Rho**	**Theta**	**Vega**	**IV**
0.95591	0.03354	0.0304	-0.00567	0.01115	0.21621	39	-0.12579	0.04994	-0.00469	-0.01394	0.02562	0.33373
0.86234	0.05757	0.0273	-0.01521	0.02701	0.30516	39.5	-0.14827	0.05773	-0.00553	-0.01506	0.02867	0.32302
0.85107	0.06728	0.02731	-0.0146	0.0285	0.2756	40	-0.17578	0.06635	-0.00656	-0.01632	0.03203	0.314
0.81668	0.0788	0.02644	-0.01617	0.03267	0.26968	40.5	-0.2091	0.07545	-0.00782	-0.0177	0.03562	0.30706
0.77493	0.09055	0.02528	-0.01781	0.03698	0.26567	41	-0.24767	0.08463	-0.00928	-0.01903	0.03917	0.30106
0.6989	0.08989	0.02272	-0.0236	0.04301	0.31126	41.5	-0.29101	0.09356	-0.01092	-0.02016	0.04247	0.29527
0.67628	0.11376	0.02239	-0.02008	0.04439	0.25386	42	-0.33871	0.10195	-0.01273	-0.02097	0.04531	0.2891
0.61763	0.12302	0.02058	-0.02081	0.04716	0.24938	42.5	-0.39159	0.10803	-0.01477	-0.0217	0.04756	0.28638
0.5546	0.12978	0.01859	-0.02106	0.04889	0.24504	43	-0.44691	0.11242	-0.0169	-0.02195	0.04895	0.28321
0.48883	0.13248	0.01646	-0.02091	0.04935	0.24233	43.5	-0.50381	0.11447	-0.01912	-0.02177	0.04937	0.28053
0.42237	0.13186	0.01429	-0.02016	0.04845	0.23902	44	-0.5606	0.11366	-0.02137	-0.02123	0.04878	0.27916
0.35661	0.12774	0.01212	-0.01883	0.04618	0.23514	44.5	-0.61522	0.11	-0.02356	-0.02038	0.04725	0.27944
0.29616	0.11891	0.0101	-0.01732	0.04281	0.23421	45	-0.68066	0.1103	-0.0261	-0.01735	0.04414	0.26032
0.2402	0.10782	0.00821	-0.01543	0.03853	0.23246	45.5	-0.71153	0.0964	-0.02758	-0.01806	0.04216	0.28449

Figure 14: BAC option Greeks (Source: NASDAQ)

Based on these criteria, we can pick the 42-strike put option with a delta of 33 and IV of 28.9%. The option premium is $1.25. Note that the 41.5 strike also fulfills our criteria; however, the option price is $1.03. So, by picking the 42-strike put, we can increase the premium income by about 25% with a marginally higher delta. Also, remember that we would like to pick a strike price below the short-term support zone (which is $43 in this case).

> **The 1% Rule:** Many options traders follow a simple rule of thumb of choosing an option whose premium is at least 1% of the stock price. So, if the stock price is $43, the minimum acceptable option premium is $0.43.

Step 4: Calculating potential returns and break-even points

So, following step 3, here is the summary of our option position:

Position summary:

◇ **Stock price**: $43.31

◇ **Strike price**: $42

◇ **Premium received**: $1.25

◇ **Expiration date**: June 20, 2025

◇ **Contract size**: 100 shares

◇ **Days to Expiration (DTE)**: 29 days

Next, we will look at how much capital we need, maximum profit, return on capital, and the break-even point.

Capital required (cash reserved to buy stock):

Capital Required = $42×100 = $4,200.

Note: $42 is the strike price. So, in case the assignment happens, you are obliged to buy 100 shares of BAC at $42 per share.

Maximum profit:

Max profit = option premium * 100 = $1.25 * 100 = $125.

This is how much you earn when the option expires worthless (BAC stays above $42).

Return on capital (ROC):

Return on capital = premium income / capital deployed * 100 = $125/4,200 * 100 = 2.98% in 29 days.

This gives us a great annualized return of over 37%!

Break-even price:

This is the effective price at which you'd own the stock in case of an assignment.

Break even = strike price - option premium = 42−1.25 = $40.75.

You'd only start to experience unrealized losses when the stock falls below $40.75 by expiry.

Step 5: Placing the order and managing the position

Following step 4, you are all set to place your first CSP trade. Now, all you need to do is log in to your brokerage account and navigate to the options trading platform or the option chain of your chosen stock.

Now, find the specific put option with your selected strike price and expiration date. Next, click on the bid price of the put option. This is the price buyers are willing to pay for the option right now. Now, select "Sell to Open", enter the number of contracts you want to sell, and set your limit price for the minimum premium you want to receive.

(**Note**: "Sell to Open" means you are opening a new short position by selling options. The other order types are "Buy to Close" or "Sell to Close.")

Finally, before placing the order, review the details carefully to confirm your stock ticker, strike price, expiration date, and number of contracts. And of course, you need to have the required cash (in the case of our BAC option, it's $4,200) in your account to get your order fulfilled. Then submit the order and keep monitoring the status. If the order doesn't get filled immediately, adjust the limit price or wait.

Congratulations, you just placed your first CSP trade.

Note: Watch a detailed explanation on how to place a CSP trade on our YouTube Channel "Oliver El-Gorr - Freeman Publications."

Wrapping it up

Executing a CSP trade needs to be a well-thought-out step-by-step process*, starting from gauging the broader market sentiment to placing an order. Once your order gets filled, your job isn't done yet. You need to monitor your trade for a few minutes every day and make necessary adjustments if required. At times, you may want to close your trade early after pocketing the larger part of the premium, while at other times, you may want to hold until expiration. You may also want to roll your position to a later expiration date or a different strike price based on the stock's movement. After all, the market is a dynamic place, and we can't have a static strategy. We will discuss all these adjustment techniques in the next chapter.

*If you need detailed, personalized, hands-on guidance with your first CSP trades, give us a call, and we can help. We work with thousands of students of all ages and help them make between $500 to $5,000 every month in passive income through CSPs. To book a free consultation, go to https://investingcoach.com/work-with-me

Key takeaways

◇ While executing CSPs, always start by analyzing the larger market sentiment. CSPs work best in a bullish or a consolidating market.

◇ Pick the right stock based on different fundamental and technical criteria.

◇ We would like to execute CSPs on stocks showing a bullish trend or bullish consolidation.

◇ Pick the right strike price and expiration date based on option premium, delta, IV, and days to expire (DTE).

◇ Calculate the payoffs, cash required, break-even point, and ROC before moving further.

◇ Double-check the sticker symbol, strike price, expiration date, and number of contracts before placing your order.

Chapter 12

MAKING ADJUSTMENTS FOR OPTIMAL RETURNS

"Sometimes you make the right decision, sometimes you make the decision right"
– Phil McGraw.

Here's a simple truth that most options books ignore: options give you options!

I know that sounds like clever wordplay, but it's actually the most important concept you'll learn about position management. When you buy stocks, your choices are limited... hold, sell, or maybe average down. But with options? You have a toolkit full of adjustment techniques that can turn potential disasters into manageable situations.

After you sell a CSP, the market might throw you curveballs. That nice uptrend could stall and reverse. Volatility might spike, making your short puts more expensive. Or (the good news scenario) your position might become profitable quickly, leaving you wondering whether to take profits or hold for maximum gain.

This chapter is your survival guide for all these scenarios.

The Best Problem to Have: When Your Trade Works Too Well

Let's start with the scenario every CSP trader loves, when the stock moves in your favor and your put starts losing value fast.

Let's say Cisco is trading at $64, and you sell the $62 put with 30 days to expiration for $1.25. A week later, Cisco jumps 5% and your put is now worth only $0.50.

You've captured $0.75 in premium (60% of the maximum possible profit) in just 7 days. The question becomes:

Should you close early and take the 60% profit, or hold for the remaining 40%?

The Math of Early Exits

Here's the reality, you just made 60% of your maximum potential return in one week. To earn that remaining 40%, you'd have to hold for another 23 days. That's a much slower rate of return on your tied-up capital.

The Early Exit Strategy

Our experience across tens of thousands of CSP trades (and one which has also been proven by numerous backtests) shows that you'll maximize profits by closing positions early in most cases.

Start with a buyback order that exits your when the option loses 50% of its value (you've captured 50% of premium), this can be valid for the first 2 weeks of the trade. After that, definitely close when you've captured 70-80% of the premium. It's not worth the risk of reversal.

Why Early Exits Work

Capital efficiency: Free up money for new trades with better risk/reward

Risk reduction: Avoid potential reversals that could erase your gains

Compounding effect: More frequent, smaller wins often beat fewer, larger wins

In bullish or sideways markets, we typically close CSP trades in 7-10 days. For context, through the entirety of 2023, my average trade length was 8.9 days.

When the Market Turns Against You: Rolling Techniques

Now for the scenarios that test your skills: when the stock drops and assignment starts looking likely.

This is where options truly give you options. Through "rolling," you can adjust your position to avoid assignment or buy yourself more time.

Rolling Explained Simply

Rolling means closing your current position and opening a new one with different terms (strike price, expiration, or both). Think of it as trading in your current option for a better one.

Rolling Down: Lowering Your Strike

Example: Intel is at $21. You sold the $20 put for $0.75 with 20 days left. Intel drops to $18.75, putting your put in the money at $1.50.

Instead of taking a $75 loss, you can roll down

◇ Buy to close the $20 put for $1.50 (debit of $150)

◇ Sell to open the $18 put for $1.10 (credit of $110)

Result: You still have a net credit of $35 ($75 original + $110 new - $150 buyback), and now the stock needs to fall further for assignment.

When to roll down - If your option is 1-4% in the money, and the stock is near a support level.

Rolling Out: Buying More Time

Example: Starbucks is at $80. You sold the $75 put for $1.25 with 21 days left. A week later, Starbucks is at $75.50 and your put is worth $1.50.

You can roll out:

◇ Buy to close the current $75 put for $1.50 (debit of $150)

◇ Sell to open a new $75 put with 30 days for $1.75 (credit of $175)

Result: You've bought more time and actually increased your total premium collected.

When to roll out: Option is near the money but not yet in it, and you believe the downturn is temporary.

Rolling Down and Out: The Nuclear Option

Example: PayPal is at $70. You sold the $66 put for $1.50 with 30 days left. Two weeks later, PayPal crashes 10% to $63, and your put is worth $4.50.

Time for the aggressive approach:

◇ Buy to close the $66 put for $4.50 (debit of $450)

◇ Sell to open a $60 put with 30-45 days for $4.00 (credit of $400)

Result: You still have a net credit position of $100, with a lower strike and more time.

When to roll down and out: Option is deep in the money, and you need both more time and a lower strike to avoid assignment.

The rolling decision matrix

Situation	Rolling method	Goal
Strike is ITM, but the stock is near support	Roll down	Lower the strike and avoid an assignment
The option is ATM/ near ITM, and the trend might reverse	Roll out	Buy time
Deep ITM and the outlook is still bearish	Roll down & out	Buy time and lower the strike

Important Rolling Warnings

Rolling isn't magic and doesn't fix every trade, for example...

◊ Rolling can create net debits (you pay more than you collect)
◊ Falling knives keep falling (fundamentally broken stocks don't recover)
◊ You might just be delaying the inevitable (and making it worse)

This is why we emphasize picking quality stocks you'd actually want to own.

When Assignment Happens

Sometimes, despite your best rolling efforts, you get assigned. What then?

If you're done everything correctly, you still own shares of a company you researched and wanted to own anyway. Here's your playbook:

◇ **Hold for the long term:** Quality large-cap stocks historically return 9-10% annually

◇ **Collect dividends:** Many CSP-worthy stocks pay dividends

Want more real examples of trades?

Check out the free video walkthroughs on our YouTube Channel, we've got real trade examples, tutorials, and interviews with successful CSP traders.

https://freemanpublications.com/youtube

And remember, assignment isn't failure... it's Plan B.

Key takeaways

◇ Options give you flexibility to adjust your positions.

◇ Think of closing a CSP position early after capturing 50–80% of the premium.

◇ Rolling down lowers your strike price to avoid assignment. However, roll down a position only when the stock's decline looks temporary.

◇ Rolling out gives your position more time to recover without changing the strike. Rolling down and out combines a lower strike and more time.

◇ Avoid rolling trades endlessly. If the fundamentals have changed for the worse, take the loss and move on.

◇ If the assignment happens, own the stock and think of switching to selling covered calls under the Wheel Strategy.

Chapter 13

MONEY MANAGEMENT... THE DIFFERENCE BETWEEN SURVIVING AND THRIVING

"Large losses are forever–in investing, in teenage driving, and in fidelity. If you avoid large losses with a strong defense, the winnings will have every opportunity to take care of themselves. And large losses are almost always caused by trying to get too much by taking too many risks."
- Charles Ellis.

There's a great X-Files episode where Fox Mulder, finds himself bedridden and face-to-face with a vampire. But Mulder knows something about vampire folklore... they're compulsively obsessed with counting. So he throws a handful of sunflower seeds on the floor. The vampire, unable to resist, starts counting every single seed. By the time he's finished, the sun has risen and the danger has passed.

The Trader's Vampire Problem

We're not vampires, but many traders have a similar compulsive behavior: they get distracted by every shiny trading opportunity that crosses their path, losing sight of their real goal... sustainable, profitable trading.

That high-premium CSP on a sketchy biotech stock? Those are your sunflower seeds. That "can't miss" opportunity on a penny stock? More seeds on the floor.

While you're busy counting (chasing every trade), you're missing the bigger picture which is building a systematic, disciplined approach to CSP trading.

This is why money management matters more than stock picking, more than technical analysis, more than understanding the Greeks. Get your money management wrong, and none of the other stuff matters.

Position Sizing: The Foundation of Everything

Let me tell you about Jake's mistake.

Jake started with $3,000 and immediately tried to run five different CSP positions on stocks under $10. His reasoning? "I want to diversify and generate maximum cash flow."

Within two months, Jake was assigned on three positions, a struggling retailer, some Chinese E-Commerce operation I'm surprised even had tradeable options, and a crypto mining stock that got caught in a downswing. His "diversified" portfolio was down 60%.

Jake's problem wasn't bad luck. It was bad money management.

The Reality of Minimum Account Size

Here's the truth, CSP trading requires real capital to work effectively. While you can technically start with less, our experience shows you need a minimum of $5,000-$10,000 to do this properly.

Why? Because this gives you access to quality stocks in the $15-$50 range. Companies like Bank of America, Verizon, KeyCorp, and Coupang... real, profitable businesses with solid fundamentals. Anything less than that and you'll generally be forced to trade garbage stocks that you'd never want to hold.

119

The Concentration Principle

When you're starting out, concentration beats diversification every time.

With a $5,000-$10,000 account, you should have no more than 2-3 CSP positions. Yes, that means putting 30-50% of your capital into each position. This might feel scary, but it's actually safer than spreading thin across low-quality stocks.

Why Concentration Works for Small Accounts

Forces quality selection: You can't afford to pick bad stocks

Easier to manage: You can actually monitor and understand your positions

Better learning: You'll understand how CSPs work without overwhelming complexity

The Diversification Evolution

As your account grows, your approach should evolve:

$5,000-$10,000: 1-2 concentrated positions

$10,000-$50,000: 2-4 positions, start sector diversification

$50,000-$100,000: 4-7 positions, start trading multiple expiry dates for weekly income

$100,000-$250,000: 7-10 positions, maximum $25,000 per stock (remember you can always trade multiple contracts)

$250,000+: 10-15 positions, go deeper on high-conviction trades

Smart Diversification Strategies

When you do diversify, do it intelligently...

Sector Diversification: Pick 3-5 strong sectors (financials, tech, healthcare, consumer goods, utilities), then select 1-2 stocks from each. This protects you from sector-specific crashes.

Time Diversification: Stagger your expiration dates. Instead of having all your CSPs expire the same week, spread them out like so...

◇ American Airlines 21 DTE $12 strike: $0.75 premium

◇ American Airlines 28 DTE $12 strike: $0.95 premium

This creates weekly cash flow and reduces the impact of short-term market moves.

Strike Diversification: Consider multiple strikes on the same stock if you have high conviction. This lets you capture different risk/reward profiles.

The Scaling Challenge

As your account grows beyond $150,000, you'll face a tempting trap: the urge to keep adding more and more positions. It feels logical, right? More money means more opportunities, which should mean more positions.

Resist this urge.

Instead of spreading your capital across 25 or 30 different CSP positions, focus on increasing position sizes on your highest-conviction trades. This is where the real money gets made... not in having the most positions, but in having the right positions sized appropriately.

Why More Isn't Always Better

There's a point where additional diversification starts working against you, and most traders don't realize when they've crossed that line.

First, there's the management overhead problem. Once you get beyond 15-20 positions, keeping track of everything becomes a full-time job. You'll spend more time managing positions than researching new opportunities. What started as a strategy to generate passive income turns into a second career that demands constant attention.

Then there's the diluted returns issue. When you spread your capital too thin across dozens of positions, your best ideas get the same allocation as your mediocre ones. If you have high conviction in five stocks but equal conviction in twenty, you're essentially betting that you can't tell the difference between good and great opportunities. That's rarely true.

Finally, consider the time commitment factor. CSPs are supposed to be a lifestyle-friendly strategy that takes maybe an hour of your day. When you're managing 30+ positions, you'll find yourself spending eight hours a day monitoring, adjusting, and stress-managing your trades. At that point, you might as well get a job at a hedge fund.

The sweet spot for most traders is 10-15 well-researched, properly-sized positions that you can manage efficiently while still maintaining the quality of life that drew you to CSP trading in the first place.

The Psychological Challenges

Money management isn't just about math... it's about psychology. And psychology is where most traders fail, even when they know all the right formulas.

I learned this lesson the hard way early in my trading career. I had calculated the "optimal" position size for a CSP trade on a tech stock. The math was perfect... 15% of my account, well within my risk parameters. But I made one crucial mistake, I ignored how I'd feel if the trade went wrong.

When the stock started dropping and my CSP moved into the money, something unexpected happened. I was checking my phone every hour, watching the position move against me. During the day, I couldn't concentrate on anything else. The stress was consuming me.

The problem wasn't that I'd risked too much money objectively... it was that I'd risked too much money for my psychological comfort level. There's a huge difference between what you can afford to lose on paper and what you can afford to lose emotionally.

This is why proper position sizing does more than protect your capital. When you size positions appropriately for your psychological makeup, you sleep better at night knowing you're not over-leveraged. You think more clearly because you're not stressed about oversized positions. And most importantly, you act rationally when adjustments are needed instead of making panic decisions.

I've seen traders with $100,000 accounts stress over $2,000 positions, and I've seen others with $20,000 accounts calmly manage $5,000 positions. The difference isn't the money... it's the person. Your position size needs to match not just your account size, but your stress tolerance.

Your Money Management Checklist

Before opening any CSP position, ask yourself:

⋄ Is this position size appropriate for my account?

⋄ Am I properly diversified across sectors and time?

⋄ Do I have cash available for adjustments?

⋄ Can I manage this number of positions effectively?

⋄ Would I be comfortable owning this stock if assigned?

The Bottom Line

Great money management won't guarantee profits, but poor money management will guarantee losses. It's the difference between building sustainable wealth and blowing up your account chasing the next shiny opportunity.

Remember: CSPs should generate steady cash flow, not constant stress. If you're losing sleep over your positions, your position sizes are too big.

In the next chapter, we'll put everything together and walk through your first CSP trade from start to finish, incorporating all the money management principles we've covered.

Chapter 14

HOW TO INCREASE YOUR ODDS OF SUCCESS

"Opportunities multiply as they are seized."
- Sun Tzu, The Art of War.

W hen Ray Dalio speaks about investing, the world listens. After all, he runs Bridgewater Associates, the world's largest hedge fund with over $124 billion in assets under management.

But in 1982, Ray Dalio was broke.

During the early days of his career, Dalio made a catastrophic prediction. He was convinced the US economy was headed for a massive recession and advised his clients to position accordingly. He couldn't have been more wrong.

What followed was the longest period of economic growth in US history. The stock market soared. Dalio lost everything.

Reflecting on this devastating period, he later wrote:

"Losing this bet was like a blow to my head with a baseball bat. I went broke and had to borrow $4,000 from my dad just to pay my family bills. Due to the losses, I was forced to lay off the people I cared so much about... until my company was left with just one employee: me."

The Turning Point

This wasn't the end of Ray Dalio's story. It was the beginning of his real education.

The failure transformed him from someone who thought "I'm right" to someone who asked "How do I know I'm right?" It made him what he calls "radically open-minded."

In his own words...

> *"But in retrospect, that failure was one of the best things that ever happened to me. It gave me the humility I needed to balance my aggressiveness."*

The Long Game Mindset

Success in CSP trading isn't about hitting home runs on individual trades. It's about consistently hitting singles and doubles over years and decades.

This requires a fundamental shift in how you think about trading. Instead of asking "How much can I make this month?" start asking "If I keep doing this consistently, where will I be in 3, 4, or 5 years?"

When you adopt this long-term perspective, everything changes. You're not desperate to take every trade that comes along. You don't panic when the VIX spikes. You don't risk money you can't afford to lose. You understand that preserving capital for the right opportunities is more important than forcing trades in poor conditions.

For instance, when the VIX climbs above 30, we tell our students to sit on their hands and do nothing. Only traders with a long-term mindset can resist the fear of missing out and the temptation to overtrade during volatile periods.

Setting Realistic Expectations

A long-term mindset doesn't mean you shouldn't have short-term milestones. Create reasonable monthly income targets based on 20-30% annual returns from CSPs. That translates to roughly 1.5-2.5% monthly returns on your capital.

Starting with a $10,000 account? Expect to generate $150-$250 per month on average. If you don't need that cash for expenses, reinvest it to accelerate your account growth.

We've seen students earning anywhere from $500 to over $50,000 per month (not a typo) depending on their account size, all while dedicating less than four hours per week to their positions.

The key is combining monthly income expectations with long-term wealth building. Reinvest your cash flows, grow your account, diversify your positions, and gradually increase position sizes as your capital grows.

The Kaizen Approach to Trading Excellence

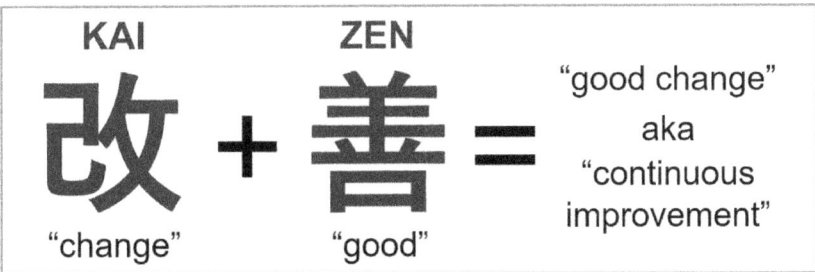

KAI + **ZEN** = "good change" aka "continuous improvement"

"change" "good"

Figure 15: Kaizen (Source: leansmarts.com)

Ever wonder why Japanese products are synonymous with quality and reliability? Think Toyota... from the humble Corolla to the sleek Camry, they've set the standard for value and innovation.

The secret lies in a Japanese philosophy called "Kaizen," which literally means "change for the better." Instead of trying to improve everything at once, Kaizen focuses on small, daily improvements that compound over time.

You can apply this same principle to your CSP trading.

CSPs might seem straightforward, but there are countless nuances to master. Every trade teaches you something about stock selection, entry timing, volatility management, or position adjustment. The market constantly presents new scenarios and challenges.

Be mindful of these lessons. Keep a trading journal. Note what worked, what didn't, and why. As James Clear demonstrates in "Atomic Habits," improving just 1% every day makes you 37 times better within a year.

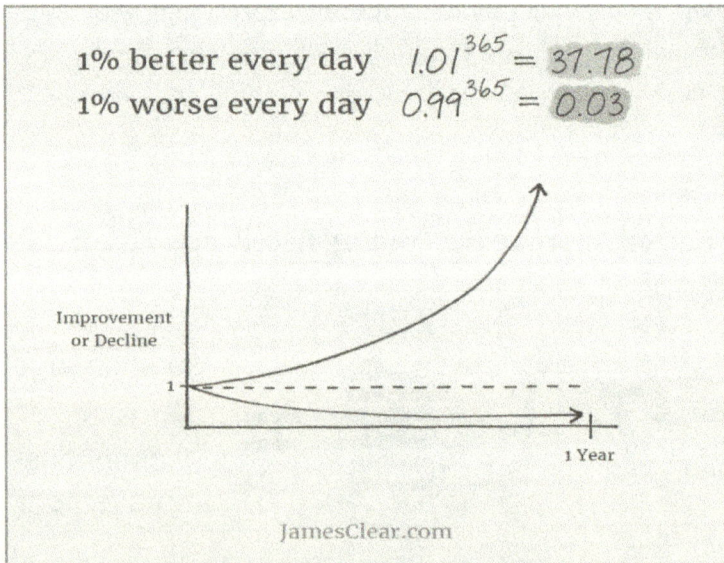

1% better every day $1.01^{365} = 37.78$
1% worse every day $0.99^{365} = 0.03$

Improvement or Decline

1

1 Year

JamesClear.com

Figure 16: The power of tiny gains (Source: jamesclear.com)

All great traders, from Ed Seykota to William Eckhardt, emphasize continuous learning. They understand that mastery isn't a destination... it's a journey of constant improvement.

The Power of Mentorship and Community

Warren Buffett had Benjamin Graham. Paul Tudor Jones had Eli Tullis. Ray Dalio learned from his devastating failure.

Every successful trader has learned from someone who walked the path before them.

As Paul Tudor Jones said about his mentor...

> *"He was the toughest son of a b**h I ever knew. He taught me that trading is very competitive and you have to be able to handle getting your butt kicked. No matter how you cut it, there are enormous emotional ups and downs involved."*

The emotional aspect of trading is often underestimated. Having mentors and a supportive community helps you navigate the psychological challenges that inevitably arise. They can share hard-won wisdom, help you avoid common pitfalls, and provide perspective during difficult periods.

While you ultimately have to do the work yourself, having guidance during your learning phase can dramatically accelerate your progress and help you avoid costly mistakes.

The Dangerous Jungle

Ray Dalio once posed this question:

> *"Imagine that in order to have a great life, you have to cross a dangerous jungle. You can stay safe where you are and have an ordinary life, or you can risk crossing the jungle to have a terrific life. How would you approach that choice?"*

The journey from ordinary to exceptional trader is much like crossing that jungle. It requires bold decisions, continuous learning, and the humility to admit when you're wrong.

But here's the thing about CSP trading: it's not actually a dangerous jungle. When done properly, with sound money management and quality stock selection, it's more like a well-marked hiking trail. There are still risks, but they're manageable with the right preparation and guidance.

Your Path Forward

Success in CSP trading comes down to three fundamental principles:

Think long-term: Focus on consistent, sustainable returns rather than quick wins. Build wealth over years and decades, not days and weeks.

Improve continuously: Embrace the Kaizen mindset. Learn something from every trade, every market condition, every success and failure.

Seek guidance: Learn from those who've walked this path before you. Whether through books, courses, mentorship, or community, leverage the experience of others to accelerate your own progress.

And remember, there are people who've successfully navigated this journey before you. You don't have to figure it all out alone.

The difference between traders who succeed and those who fail isn't intelligence, luck, or even starting capital. It's the willingness to think long-term, learn continuously, and seek guidance from those who've already achieved what you're trying to accomplish.

If you're ready to take your CSP trading to the next level with proper guidance and support, we're here to help.

To schedule a conversation about whether our program might be a good fit for you, visit: https://investingcoach.com/work-with-me

Key takeaways

◇ Have monthly income targets, but build a long-term investing mindset to excel in CSPs.

◇ Reinvest your earnings to grow your account faster.

◇ Focus on continuous learning from mistakes, keep a trading journal, and improve your trades over time.

◇ Access to mentorship and a learning community can help you become a more profitable trader.

Chapter 15

THE WHEEL STRATEGY... WHEN CSPS MEET THEIR PERFECT PARTNER

"If opportunity doesn't knock, build a door."
- **Milton Berle.**

In Chinese philosophy, there's a beautiful concept called Yin and Yang. Two opposite forces that complement each other perfectly, creating balance and harmony in the universe.

Options trading has its own version of Yin and Yang, and when you combine them, something magical happens. You create what's known as the Wheel Strategy... a complete, balanced approach that keeps cash flowing regardless of what the market throws at you.

The Perfect Partnership

You already know the Yin, Cash Secured Puts (CSPs). You've learned how to generate steady income by selling puts on quality stocks you'd be happy to own.

Now meet the Yang, Covered Calls (CCs). This is the strategy that perfectly complements CSPs, creating a circular system where your capital never sits idle.

Here's the beautiful thing about the Wheel, you don't need to change anything about how you're already trading CSPs. You simply add this second component when the situation calls for it.

What Is a Covered Call?

A covered call is CSPs' mirror image. Instead of selling puts while holding cash, you sell calls while holding stock.

Let's say you own 100 shares of a stock, and you sell a call option against those shares. If the call expires worthless, you keep the premium. If the call gets exercised, you sell your shares at the strike price.

The key word here is "covered." You're covered because you actually own the stock. This is the opposite of selling "naked" calls, which is essentially financial suicide. With naked calls, if the stock skyrockets, you'd have to buy shares at market price to deliver them at the strike price. That's a recipe for unlimited losses.

A Real-World Example

Let's say you own 100 shares of Johnson & Johnson (JNJ), currently trading at $155. The stock has been moving sideways, and you think it'll stay in that range for a while.

You decide to sell a $160 call option for $1.60, collecting $160 in premium.

Two scenarios can play out...

Scenario 1: JNJ stays below $160 at expiration. You keep the $160 premium, and you still own your shares. You can sell another call next month.

Scenario 2: JNJ rises above $160. Your shares get called away at $160, and you keep the $160 premium. You've made money on both the stock appreciation ($5 per share) and the premium income.

The Missing Piece

Now here's where covered calls become the perfect partner for CSPs.

Remember what happens when you get assigned on a CSP? You suddenly own 100 shares of stock, but your premium income stops. Your capital is tied up in shares that might take weeks or months to recover to profitable selling levels.

This is where most CSP traders get stuck. They're holding stock, earning maybe a small dividend, but missing out on the premium income that drew them to options in the first place. Covered calls solve this problem.

The Wheel in Motion

The Wheel Strategy creates a continuous cycle that keeps your capital working regardless of market direction:

Phase 1: The CSP Phase - You sell cash-secured puts on a quality stock, collecting premium income. You keep doing this until you eventually get assigned and own the shares.

Phase 2: The Covered Call Phase - Now that you own the stock, you start selling covered calls against your shares. You collect premium income while waiting for the stock to recover. Eventually, one of your calls gets exercised and your shares are called away.

Phase 3: Back to the Beginning - Your capital is free again. You return to Phase 1 and start selling CSPs.

This creates a "wheel" that keeps turning, generating premium income in both directions. When you're bullish on a stock, you sell puts. When you own the stock, you sell calls. Your capital never sits idle.

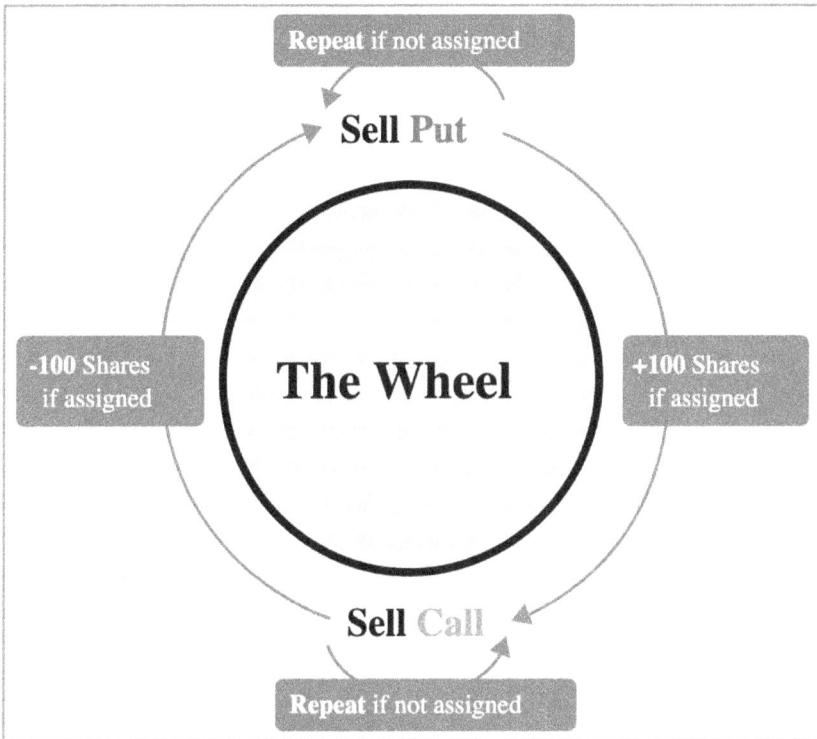

Figure 17: The options wheel strategy (Source: optionstrat.com)

The Beauty of the System

What makes the Wheel Strategy so powerful is its adaptability. You're not fighting the market or trying to predict direction. You're simply responding to what the market gives you.

Stock going up? Great, your CSPs expire worthless and you keep the premium

Stock going down? Fine, you get assigned shares of a company you wanted to own anyway

Stock moving sideways while you own it? Perfect, you sell covered calls and collect premium while you wait

The Mindset Shift

The Wheel Strategy requires a fundamental shift in how you think about trading. Instead of trying to be right about market direction, you focus on generating consistent income regardless of direction. You stop caring whether you own the stock or own cash because both positions can generate income. You stop worrying about getting assigned because assignment just moves you to the next phase of the wheel.

The Wheel in Action: A Real-World Example

Let me show you exactly how this works with a real trade.

Remember the Bank of America CSP we discussed in Chapter 11? Let's follow that trade through a complete wheel cycle:

Phase 1: The CSP Setup

◇ BAC stock price: $43.31

◇ Strike price: $42

◇ Premium received: $1.25

◇ Days to expiration: 29 days

◇ Capital required: $4,200

Phase 2: Assignment Happens - At expiration, BAC drops to $40. Your put finishes in the money, and you're assigned 100 shares at $42 each. You now own $4,200 worth of BAC stock that's currently worth $4,000.

Most traders would panic at this point. You're down $200 on paper, and your premium income has stopped.

But you're not most traders. You're a Wheel trader.

Phase 3: The Covered Call Phase - Now that you own the stock, you immediately start selling covered calls. You notice the BAC $45 call with 30 days to expiration is trading for $1.45.

You sell that call and collect another $145 in premium.

Think about what just happened: You collected $125 from the original put, and now you've collected another $145 from the call. That's $270 in total premium income on a $4,200 investment... and you're not done yet.

Phase 4: The Stock Recovers - Over the next few weeks, BAC recovers. The stock climbs to $48, putting your $45 call in the money. You get assigned again, but this time you're selling your shares.

You sell your 100 shares at $45 each, receiving $4,500.

Let's add up what happened...

◇ Original investment: $4,200 (buying shares at $42)
◇ Sale proceeds: $4,500 (selling shares at $45)
◇ Stock profit: $300
◇ Total premium collected: $270 ($125 + $145)
◇ Total profit: $570 on a $4,200 investment

That's a 13.6% return, and your capital is now free to start the wheel again.

Creating a Continuous Income Cycle

This is where the Wheel Strategy becomes truly powerful. You're never "stuck" in any position. You're always generating income, whether you own cash or stock.

When you own cash, you sell puts and collect premium. When you own stock, you sell calls and collect premium. The wheel keeps turning, and the income keeps flowing.

The Income Multiplication Effect

Here's something most traders don't realize: the Wheel can potentially double your returns compared to CSPs alone.

With standalone CSPs, when you get assigned, your capital sits in stock earning maybe a small dividend while you wait for recovery. That could be weeks or months of lost premium income.

With the Wheel, that "dead time" becomes productive time. You're collecting covered call premiums while you wait for the stock to recover. Your capital never stops working.

The Psychological Advantage

The Wheel Strategy also provides a huge psychological benefit: it eliminates the fear of assignment.

Most CSP traders dread getting assigned because it feels like failure. With the Wheel mindset, assignment is just the next phase of your strategy. You're not stuck... you're transitioning.

This mental shift is liberating as you stop trying to avoid assignment and start focusing on what really matters, generating consistent income regardless of market direction.

The Learning Curve Advantage

Here's the best part about adding covered calls to your CSP arsenal, there's almost no additional learning curve.

Everything you've learned about strike selection, volatility management, the Greeks, and rolling techniques applies to covered calls too. You're not starting from scratch... you're building on knowledge you already have. So the same principles that make you successful with CSPs will make you successful with covered calls...

◇ Choose quality stocks you want to own

◇ Select appropriate strike prices and expiration dates

◇ Manage positions actively

◇ Use rolling techniques when needed

The Most Effective Income Strategy I know

The Wheel Strategy isn't just about making more money (though it certainly does that). It's about creating a complete system that works in any market environment.

Bull market? Your puts expire worthless and your calls get exercised at higher prices. Bear market? You get assigned quality stocks at discounted prices and sell calls while you wait for recovery. Sideways market? You collect premium from both puts and calls as the stock trades in a range.

You become market-direction agnostic. Instead of trying to predict where stocks are going, you profit from wherever they actually go.

Getting Started

If you're ready to take your CSP trading to the next level and implement the complete Wheel Strategy, remember that the right guidance can make all the difference.

While covered calls share many similarities with CSPs, there are nuances and advanced techniques that can significantly impact your results. Having experienced mentors to guide you through the learning process can help you avoid costly mistakes and accelerate your progress.

If you'd like step-by-step guidance on mastering covered calls and implementing the complete Wheel Strategy, we're here to help. To schedule a free consultation and see if our coaching program might be right for you, visit: https://investingcoach.com/work-with-me

The Wheel Strategy has the potential to transform your approach to income generation. It's not just about trading options... it's about creating financial freedom through consistent, predictable cash flow.

Key takeaways

◇ You can combine CSPs with CCs to create a solid options strategy called the Wheel Strategy.

◇ The Wheel involves cyclically selling CSPs and CCs to keep them continuously generating income, irrespective of whether the stock is assigned.

◇ The Wheel can potentially double your premium income by preventing your capital from lying idle.

CONCLUSION

In 2020, a Northwestern Mutual survey revealed that the average American needed about $951,000 in savings for a comfy retirement. In the 2024 survey, the magic number jumped by 53% to $1.46 million. Going by this trend, expect your goalpost to shift miles towards the north in the next 4-5 years. The retirement math isn't getting any easier day by day.

Even if you manage this herculean task of saving $1.5-$2 million in the next decade or so, do you think your job is done? Ask any retiree about how it feels to look at their dwindling savings when there are not enough cash inflows to replenish them. It's not a pleasant scene. Expect expenses to go up steadily, and the approach of having a fixed savings target for a comfortable retirement is not going to work. (Did it ever work at all?). Plus, no one likes to dig into their savings to pay for living expenses. This means one thing: **Income is king**.

A comfortable retirement is about how much income you can consistently generate without eating into your savings. The conventional options of putting your money to work through high-yield savings or dividend investing don't work either. At best, they can help you beat inflation. That's much like running on a treadmill: a lot of effort with no forward motion. You are working hard just to be in the same place. It's time to take an unconventional approach to retirement planning while keeping risks low. This is where CSPs fit in.

Options often don't go well with a low-risk retirement strategy, mainly because they have a bad reputation for "excessive risks." The reality, however, is that much of the risks associated with options come from not knowing what you are doing. Options can be used in ways that generate a regular income while keeping the risk level within your

141

comfort zone. A CSP is a low-risk options strategy that solves two goals, generating a regular income and acquiring stocks at a lower price. In that sense, CSPs combine the power of income generation and value investing.

With low-risk CSPs, our students generate a monthly income of $500 to $5,000, depending on their account sizes. You can give a boost to your CSP income by combining it with the Wheel Strategy.

Yes, both the CSP and the Wheel Strategy can be executed on your own if you follow a step-by-step learning approach. Master the basics first, start small, learn from your mistakes, and follow the learning curve to improve your trades. Mentorship programs can accelerate your learning, help you avoid common mistakes, and guide you through real-world scenarios that Reddit and YouTube videos often miss. Remember that making some quick bucks is not your goal. You want to build a system that generates reliable income month after month, even in retirement. Anyone can profit from a single trade by mere luck. But repeating the process every week and every month, year after year, requires some solid learning.

To allow us to guide you through all the steps in executing CSPs, starting from clearing the basics to managing your trades, get in touch with us at:

https://investingcoach.com/work-with-me

ADDITIONAL RESOURCES TO HELP YOU

To help you implement the strategies in this book, we've put together a curated set of tools, videos, and checklists to support your journey — whether you're just getting started or ready to scale up.

Free Tools & Checklists

Download trade planning templates, broker comparison charts, CSP risk calculators, and our premium watchlist at:

freemanpublications.com/bonus

Video Tutorials & Case Studies

Prefer to watch instead of read?

Explore our most popular tutorials, including:

◇ How to place your first CSP trade

◇ Mistakes to avoid with small accounts

◇ Case studies from real traders using this strategy

Subscribe here:

freemanpublications.com/youtube

1-on-1 Help With Your Portfolio

If you'd like personal guidance implementing this strategy inside your account, including help with stock selection, strike price targeting, and rolling positions, book a free call with me or my team:

https://investingcoach.com/work-with-me

WHY I STARTED
FREEMAN PUBLICATIONS

My introduction to investing was watching my grandfather lose almost everything in the 2008 crash. Despite being a war hero, multi-lingual and a successful businessman - he fell foul of bad advice and saw his portfolio crumble in the Global Financial Crisis. That sparked my lifelong learning journey with the goal of avoiding the mistakes he made.

I found that most investing-focused content spent too much time focusing on the minutia or what I call the spreadsheet-side of investing, and very little on the human element. Thus being fundamentally inaccessible to the average person.

My goal with these books is to explain financial concepts in plain English, with real examples so that you can apply the information in your own portfolio. That is because I truly believe the average individual investor is better equipped to "beat the market" long term than most Wall Street professionals.

I also wants these books to be something that pass down through multiple generations, since I became a father in 2024, I now think with an even longer time horizon. I hope one day my daughter will be in a better financial position than me, but that all starts with having the right knowledge.

That's why Freeman Publications exists.

Oliver El-Gorr

REFERENCES

◇ *[WSJ article - robinhood touts rock-bottom fees for options trading. then come the hidden costs] - bogleheads.org.* Available at: https://www. bogleheads.org/forum/viewtopic.php?t=439833 (Accessed: 03 June 2025).

◇ *Here's how much Americans say they need to retire - and it's 53% higher than four years ago. CBS News.* Available at: https://www.cbsnews. com/news/retirement-savings-how-much-americans-need-1-46-million/ (Accessed: 03 June 2025).

◇ *How Buffett used 'financial weapons of mass destruction' to make billions of dollars. Yahoo! Finance.* Available at: https://finance.yahoo.com/ news/how-buffett-used--financial-weapons-of-mass-destruction--to-make-billions-of-dollars-175922498.html?(Accessed: 03 June 2025).

◇ Lastiri, L. (2023) *How Thales' olive bet shaped modern financial theories, Earn2Trade Blog.* Available at: https://www.earn2trade.com/blog/ thales-olive-bet/ (Accessed: 03 June 2025).

◇ Murray, A. (2024) *The IRS is testing a free method to directly file taxes. but not everyone is thrilled., Colorado Newsline.* Available at: https:// coloradonewsline.com/2024/04/06/irs-free-method-file-taxes/ (Accessed: 03 June 2025).

◇ *Nicolas Darvas made $2,000,000 using trend following methods* (2018) *Trend Following Trading Systems from Michael Covel.* Available at: https://www.trendfollowing.com/nicolas-darvas/ (Accessed: 03 June 2025).

◇ *Peloton: Will the 'netflix of fitness' succeed despite disappointing ipo? Bocconi Students Capital Markets.* Available at: https:// www.bscapitalmarkets.com/peloton-will-the-ldquonetflix-offitnessrdquo-succeed-despite-disappointing-ipo.html (Accessed: 03 June 2025).

⬦ RayDalio (2021) *Billionaire Ray Dalio on his big bet that failed: 'I went broke and had to borrow $4,000 from my dad'*, CNBC. Available at: https://www.cnbc.com/2019/12/04/billionaire-ray-dalio-was-once-broke-and-borrowed-money-from-his-dad-to-pay-family-bills.html (Accessed: 03 June 2025).

⬦ *Saving for retirement, Vanguard.* Available at: https://investor.vanguard.com/investor-resources-education/retirement/savings#:~:text=Average%20retirement%20savings,as%20of%20year%2Dend%202023. (Accessed: 03 June 2025).

⬦ *The 'liberation day' effect: Market fallout explained, tastylive.* Available at: https://www.tastylive.com/news-insights/liberation-day-effect-market-fallout-explained (Accessed: 03 June 2025).